Randy!
Thanks for
the invite!
Bill Davis #69

HIGH TIDE

*A Story of Football, Freefall,
and Forgiveness*

Jan. 29:11

Book Design by Sam Torode

ISBN-13: 978-1482762969
ISBN-10: 148276296X

Printed in the United States of America

HIGH TIDE

A STORY OF FOOTBALL, FREEFALL, AND FORGIVENESS

BILL SEARCEY

with KELLY WITTMANN

Call unto me, and I will answer thee,
and show thee great and mighty things,
which thou knowest not.
—Jeremiah 33:3

For my son Woody—the best son a dad could hope for.
Though I love you more than words could ever say,
I at least hope this book will keep you headed in the right direction
and off the path I was once taking.

CHAPTER ONE

MY LOWEST POINT? My "rock bottom"? It's really impossible to say. It could have been any one of dozens—maybe hundreds—of days, spanning across the years, the decades. So I'll just reach back into my memory and pluck one out for you as a lone example in a sea of drug-induced insanity. If it was not the very lowest, I'm sure you'll agree that it was low enough.

It was a Sunday morning in July, 2005. It was "Alabama hot," but the heat was the least of my problems. I was exiting a lovely home on the outskirts of Birmingham after spending the last two nights there. It was a pretty, white farmhouse with a whitewashed fence and a peaceful lake out front. I'd refurbished it with my ex-wife. It was rehabbed, you might say. My own rehab hadn't taken—I'd fallen back into substance abuse after a ten-year sobriety—but my home's rehab had fared much better. Except it wasn't my home any longer, and my ex-wife and thirteen-year-old son would be returning that day. They had no idea I'd been there, so I had to make tracks. I had broken into what was once my own house for a weekend of activities that had once been common for me: sleeping in a real bed, taking a real shower, etc.

Not that my ex-wife, Karen, wouldn't find me out anyway. I'd accidentally shattered a window getting in, and she'd probably guess it was me who'd done it. I'd shattered things far more precious than some easily-replaceable window, after all: Trust. Vows. Hearts. But I could break windows, too. I could break just about anything by that time.

Leaving by the front door, I walked around the back of the garage to the out-of-sight area where I'd parked my new home: a 1991 Mercury Marquis. Karen had bought it for me when she'd finally had enough of rehabs, psych wards, and my freeloading and kicked me out. I lived there now, in the backseat, when I couldn't flop at a fellow junkie's place or sneak into the upper level of the clubhouse used by my son's Little League team. There were no other options. My parents were dead. I had no siblings. I was too wracked with shame to approach the friends who had known me when I was "normal." And my former teammates?

Yeah… My former teammates, the men I'd grown so close to as an offensive lineman in the football program at the University of Alabama, or when we played together in the USFL or NFL. What on earth would they think of me now, a 400-something-pound, homeless drug addict? I would have rather died than let them know. When you're that low and desperate, you imagine that everyone from your past is a shining example of sanity and success. It isn't true, of course; I'm sure many of my former teammates were wrestling with their own demons and their own problems. But it's highly unlikely that their circumstances were as obvious and extreme as my own.

I got into the Marquis and started driving. I figured I'd return that evening, to take my lumps for the broken window and perhaps sleep in my car in what had once been my driveway (something I did on an occasional basis). And most importantly, to say goodnight to my 14-year-old son, Woody. Even at that point, I tried to remain in daily contact with him. To my great discredit, however, there were times when money for drugs cut into money for cell phone minutes or gas. On those nights, Woody had no father to say goodnight to him.

To be honest, I don't remember what happened that day in between my departure and my return, but I don't have to remember: I know. I know because the same damn thing happened every day during that time period. I was addicted to a narcotic pain pill called Lortab. 30 pills a day, 10 mg. a pill, ten pills at a time, three times a day. That's what I needed. If I didn't have those 30 pills a day, the sickness would envelop me like a wet blanket:

diarrhea, muscle and joint pain, excessive sweating, mental anguish, hellish depression. My life now was about nothing but beating that monster back. So every day consisted of the same frantic, exhausting routine.

In order to get the pills, I had to be sick. Not dope sick, but "really sick." I conveniently had two tiny kidney stones that had never passed, and I hoped they never would pass. They were an easy, go-to excuse to get Lortab every single day. If the doctors sprang a CT scan on me, I was ready; my stones were there. But I needed a little help in the symptoms department. Back then, ephedrine was still available over the counter, so if I had a few extra bucks, I'd chow some down to raise my blood pressure. Then, right before I walked into an ER or doctor's office, I'd get out my pack of cigarettes and smoke three or four in a row for good measure. Hopped up and sweating like a pig, I was all ready to go.

In the ER, they'd almost always want a urine sample. And that urine sample had to have blood in it. A prick of the finger solved that problem. Sometimes they'd do a CT scan, sometimes not. I had no insurance, so at about $2500 a scan, I was racking up quite a bit of debt, but I was past caring. The only thing that mattered was the next prescription. The only day I could concentrate on was that day. How ironic that in both my addiction and my sobriety, the constant mantra has been, "One day at a time."

Once the prescription was obtained, I would go to one of the local grocery, drug, or big discount stores. At a drug store, I'd pull the "glasses scam." Snagging one pair of reading glasses and one pair of sunglasses, I'd make small scratches on the lenses of each, then head for the customer service area. "Uh, yes... My wife bought these yesterday, but they're both scratched, so I'd like to return them, please." I might be wolfing down some food I'd stolen off the shelves even as I said this.

"You got a receipt?" an employee would reply.

"Oh, gosh, no. The wife has it. It was just crazy around the house this morning, and she forgot to give it to me. I don't need cash or anything. Just a gift card would be..."

"Yeah, all right. But next time, remember that receipt."

"Oh, I will; yes, sir."

And then there were the big discount stores. I'd walk in and hold my own cell phone up for the elderly greeter to observe. "Yeah, I need to return this."

The elderly greeter would slap a little sticker on it as an "okay" to customer service. In a matter of minutes, that little sticker would have a new home on an expensive item which I would then carry, pull, or roll over to customer service. They didn't just hand out cash, but no worries. In my most soothing voice, I'd assure them that a gift card would be fine, just fine. And it was, because gift cards could be used at their pharmacies, and the pharmacy was always my next stop. Success at last. 30 shiny, new Lortabs.

Obtaining my drug every day was a long, involved process. It was hard work. Harder than most "straight" jobs that are out there. And it became more difficult all the time. I mean, this was not some vast metropolis we're talking about; this was Birmingham, Alabama. There were only so many emergency rooms. There were only so many doctors' offices. There were only so many stores. The computer systems at the pharmacies were catching up with me. Soon, I'd be recognized all over town for what I was. Soon, I'd have a pharmacist up in my face, scolding me about the ten doctors I had in my records. Soon, technology would drive me into the streets, the last place I could buy my dope.

But with what money? There was nothing left to pawn. I'd pawned my ex-wife's wedding band and our wedding silver. I'd pawned a Rolex and several watches I'd received for playing in college bowl games. I'd even pawned my two national championship rings—*twice* (Karen had bought them back for me as a Christmas present after the first time). With nothing of value left, I'd eventually asked one of my drug buddies to rob a bank with me. He just laughed and said, "Bill, how many 400-pound bank robbers are running around Birmingham? You really think you're gonna get away with that crap?"

So, my apologies for not giving you the exact details of that day in July, 2005, but you get the picture. Now, I *do* remember returning to my former home that evening. That part is kind of hard to forget, because there were police cars in the driveway and through the family room window I could see Karen and Woody crying.

An officer approached me. "Were you here earlier?"

"Yes."

"Did you break that window in back?"

"Yes, but…"

I was immediately arrested for burglary. Karen had been worried about the broken window and had called the cops. I couldn't understand why she hadn't just assumed it was me, or maybe she did. But once I showed up and the cops slapped the cuffs on me, she asked them to reduce the charge to trespassing. They politely declined and hauled me off to jail.

There I sat in a cell with nothing, nothing. Not even my last and only friend, Lortab. The nausea would be coming on soon. I thought of my father, my mother. I thought of my hometown, Savannah, too; that place where everybody knew everybody and you couldn't hide a thing. And I knew I couldn't hide from my past when my past was inside me, pumping a ragged, irregular beat against the walls of fat and concrete that surrounded me.

CHAPTER TWO

I GUESS "QUAINT" wouldn't be the word that comes to most people's minds when they think of Savannah. At least not since *Midnight in the Garden of Good and Evil* became a publishing phenomenon. But having been born there in 1958, and having spent my entire childhood there, it's hard for me to think of it as gothic or exotic. Running through the narrow, three-story, historic-district home of my maternal grandparents, my cousins and I were more entertained than frightened by the ghosts we were sure we spotted every now and then. And that was when we weren't playing amongst the half-ruined, moss-covered gravestones in the colonial-era cemetery across the street. "Southern gothic" wasn't a phrase we learned in literature class, or a lifestyle we aspired to after thumbing through an architectural magazine; it was just life, everyday life.

Savannah at that time was a strange brew of sophisticated decadence, religious confusion, and stubborn racism. Being a port city, it had always been a melting pot that attracted adventurers, artists, and just plain weirdoes from all across the globe. At times, it has seemed like everyone who's running away from anything, whether personal, professional, or legal, has somehow wound up there. It's therefore really no wonder that very few cities in America can boast the number and variety of home-grown eccentrics that Savannah can. But as a kid, these people didn't strike me as out of the ordinary. They were just the folks my dad and I passed on our many strolls down cobblestone streets, through the beautiful downtown squares with their statues of such giants as Georgia's founder George Oglethorpe and Methodism's founder John Wesley staring silently down at us.

When I was born, my dad, William Searcey, Sr., was a young, struggling lawyer. I never felt poor as a child, but I look back now and realize that we didn't have a whole heck of a lot. We lived on New Mexico Street, in a blue-collar neighborhood, in a tiny, matchbox-type home with two bedrooms and an old floor furnace that could really burn your feet if you weren't careful on a half-conscious trip to the bathroom at night. Our home was always clean—always—but it was simple and spare, decorated with used furniture handed down by relatives or found in resale shops. The big evergreen on the front lawn was one of the very few big things we ever owned during my early childhood.

Speaking of the front lawn, I realized at a very young age that trees weren't the only thing on some southern lawns in the 1960s. My father was not only a lawyer, but an outspoken civil rights activist who angered many, many people with his insistence that black Americans deserved full and equal rights in every part of our country. Unlike some "tolerant" white southerners, who were content to sit back and wait for eventual change, Dad urged Blacks to demand their rights immediately, and he was willing to put his own life on the line, too. As his work with the NAACP became well known in the area, not just he but his whole family became the target of threats from the Ku Klux Klan and other vicious racists. I can remember police squad cars—the old "black and whites," ironically—outside our home in the dead of night, sirens wailing, lights flashing, and officers warning us that yet another nutcase had threatened to burn a cross on our lawn. I would imagine that not all of those officers were exactly sympathetic to our plight, but they showed up and they did their jobs.

Dad's parents—a merchant marine and the bride he'd found in Liverpool, England—lived right across the street from us, and I'm sure they found all this turmoil disturbing and upsetting. Others criticized Dad for bringing his wife and kid into the cause, but think about it: How can any injustice be righted otherwise? Should only single, childless people fight for such things, so as not to put any children in harm's way, ever? Of course not. Dad had his faults, but I am nothing but proud of his civil rights work, and his absolute refusal to back down in the face of threats of violence. His courage was not only respected by his many friends, but was also something that eventually won over some who swore they would never surrender to integration. And his persistence and perseverance were a big reason that this crusading lawyer was elected to the state senate from District 2, when I was just five years old.

Mom and I had helped him campaign. We made signs and went door to door to talk to the voters. We went on TV to be interviewed and stood by my father's side as he answered questions from reporters. It was my first exposure to public life, and I think I was intrigued by the camera right from the start. Though a part of me was happy to stand on the sidelines while Dad was the focus of all the attention, I think another part of me looked forward to the day when I would take center stage. I watched and learned.

For the next nine years, Dad was very busy in Atlanta with his work, and he did his work well. An extremely intelligent, even brilliant, man with a photographic memory, he always came prepared and was known for his eloquent, impassioned speeches on the floor of the senate. I was lucky enough to witness some of those speeches, and I like to think I inherited a little of his talent. Though I may not have been as outgoing as a small child as I would later become, I had been taught good southern manners—"yes, sir; no, sir"—and I felt comfortable meeting the powerful adults in my father's political circles.

Segregationist Lester Maddox became the Democratic governor a few years after Dad was elected to the senate as a Democrat. Back then, practically everyone in Georgia—whether conservative, moderate, or liberal—was a Democrat. There wasn't even a Republican primary in the 1966 election, so what does that tell you? What we were witnessing in Georgia at that time was a struggle for the soul of the Democratic Party. Jimmy Carter, a colleague of my father's in the senate, already had his eye on the governorship. But change was slow—far too slow for Dad's tastes—and you'd better believe he let everyone know it. Just as he had stood up to the racists in Savannah, he stood up to his political opponents in Atlanta and flat-out told them they were on the wrong side of history.

In other ways, however, Dad was very much a man of his time and place, and nothing is more illustrative of that than this article from the *Rome News-Tribune*, dated February 10, 1966: "The Senate also... passed a watered-down measure aimed at banning nudist colonies from Georgia... On the suggestion of Sen. Julian Webb of Donalsonville, ladies were strongly urged to leave the Senate chamber and Sen. John Gaynor of Brunswick, who was presiding, asked the doorkeeper to close the outer doors when the anti-nudist bill was called for debate. Webb noted that the bill by Sen. Roscoe Dean of Jesup contained language that 'might be offensive' to the ladies. Even the lady reading clerk departed, with her chores taken over by Sen. William Searcey of Savannah." Now that's an old-fashioned, southern gentleman!

Back home in Savannah, my mother, Lorise, was my primary caregiver, and as I was an only child, we became very close. Mom was soft-hearted, kind, and a peacemaker; the type who would literally give the shirt off her back to someone who had less than she did. When several of my cousins found themselves in a dysfunctional domestic situation, she took them in and cared for them as if they were her own. Every once in a while, she'd put us in the car and we'd take off for the coastal islands. Tybee Island was only about 20 minutes from Savannah, so most often we'd wind up there. If we had more time, we might head to Daufuskie Island, off South Carolina, which at that time was a mysterious and undeveloped place. The natives were the descendants of some of the first Blacks freed after the Civil War, and through their isolated way of living, they had preserved much of their African and Creole heritage. They even spoke their own language, called "Gullah." Together with the Gullah people, we would catch and boil shrimp and crabs, then head home with our bellies full.

My belly was full a lot back then, and I was an overweight kid. The upside of being an only child is that you rake in all the presents on Christmas morning. However, there's a downside, too. You're the focus of all your parents' love, but you're also the focus of all their criticism. My father wasn't around a lot in those years, but when he was, he could be very difficult to deal with. He was never physically abusive to either me or my mom, but I would have to say he was verbally and emotionally abusive to us both. Dad drank a lot, and when drunk, he'd sharply reprimand me for my less-than-stellar academic record and my weight. I know I could have worked harder in school, but I don't know how a young child could be expected to lose weight in 1960s Savannah. All those southern-fried, unhealthy recipes that my fellow Savannahian Paula Deen is criticized about these days? Well, back then, no one was criticizing; biscuits, gravy, fatty meats, and sugary desserts were our lifeblood.

When he came home on weekends, Dad's schedule consisted of two activities: golfing and drinking. Back in the *Mad Men* era, golf wasn't just a game. It was an important networking activity for politicians and business-men alike, and no one could work it like my father. After nine or eighteen holes, it was off to the bars. Dad's favorite bar in Savannah was a place on Victory Drive called Gildea's. Sometimes he would take me out to "run errands" and we'd just happen to wind up outside Gildea's or one of his other hangouts. Dad would leave me alone in his enormous Chrysler for hours as he drank and played pool with his buddies. I know it sounds shocking these days, but back then it really didn't seem like a big deal to anyone. The culture of gentlemanly drinking was accepted and even cel-ebrated in Savannah (never more so than in the weeks surrounding St. Patrick's Day, when Savannahians would behave… well, not so gentle-manly). And how could it hurt a kid to sit and listen to a car radio for an afternoon? Still, as I got older, I got bored with it, and started wandering into these pubs to play with the big boys. They'd put me up on a bar stool and order me a cherry Coke, and I'd listen to all the B.S.-ing and raucous laughter. I'd be lying if I said it was never fun.

From outside appearances, it may have seemed that Dad never "paid" for his drinking. After all, he knew almost every cop in both Savannah and Atlanta, and if one who *didn't* know him pulled him over when he was a little tipsy, a flash of his credentials was all it took for him to be on his merry way. Mom may have disapproved of his partying, but she didn't give him enough grief to make him quit, and certainly never threatened to leave him. And if he and his drinking buddies were planning to get really loaded on the golf course, he'd think nothing of bringing his kid—me—along to drive the golf cart. We just didn't live in a recovery culture back then, and there were no confrontations, no interventions. Yet I believe Dad did pay for his drinking, suffering inside. In his forties, depression got a grip on him.

I've wondered which current treatments might have helped him: talk therapy, anti-depressants, vigorous exercise, perhaps even the cathartic experience of writing a book, as I'm doing now. As for religion, well, I just don't think it ever happened for him. Dad was Mr. Rationality, a man whose whole life revolved around facts, science, and evidence. If he couldn't see it, feel it, smell it, taste it… then it just didn't exist. Mom, who came from a large, Lebanese-Catholic family, had converted to Episcopalism when she married Dad, and when I was small, we attended mass regularly at St. John's Episcopal Church, the largest and wealthiest parish in the diocese of Georgia. But there soon came a time when Dad refused to go inside St. John's during services; he just stood outside smoking cigarette after cigarette. Soon we stopped going to mass except for Christmas and Easter. Then we stopped going to mass at all. I was too young to understand why back then, but I've since learned that the church's rector at the time, the Reverend Ernest Risley, refused to allow Blacks to attend mass at St. John's. As mind-boggling as it seems now, in 1965 he told *Time* magazine, "I believe that integration is contrary to God's will." How sad that bigots like this man drove my father and many other people away from the church (though I'm happy to report that Risley was eventually deposed from the priesthood).

I may not have known about the racial controversy at our family's church, but by my middle school years I sure was aware of racial tensions at my school, Myers Junior High. Busing for integration had begun, and there were constant arguments and even physical altercations between black and white students. That was a source of stress for me, as was my continuing weight problem. My three best buddies—Gary, Mark, and Tiger—seemed to all at once be acquiring girlfriends, but girls weren't interested in me. Still, I did have plenty of fun in those years, both "good, clean fun" and the other kind. When my friends and I weren't riding bicycles, zooming around in go-carts, or building forts in the woods, we were hitch-hiking, drinking beer, and smoking pot. The drinking and cigarettes started at around age 12. Go ahead and gasp, but again, at the time, it was like, "No big whoop."

I began playing organized sports at a young age, but to be honest, things didn't start out very promisingly. I was "just okay" at football and baseball, and please don't even ask me about basketball. I kept at it, but even football wasn't exactly my idea of a good time, for the simple reason that I just didn't excel at it. It was a good way to make friends, however, and though I was no gridiron star back then, I wasn't a total loser, either. I had about an average amount of friends for a kid that age, and I do believe that the positives of organized sports outweighed the negatives, at least for me. I know it sounds cliché to say that athletics "builds character," but it can instill a sense of hope that a child will able to call on later in life. Whether it's football or tennis, whether it's a team sport or an individual sport, whether the participants are boys or girls, the lesson is universal: There will always be another play, another round, another game. Second chances—and third, and fourth—are everywhere in life, if only we will look for them and take advantage of them.

In addition to my human friends, I always had one or two dog friends hanging around. I particularly remember Sissy, a boxer who loved taking chances as much as I did. Sissy would chase car after car down New Mexico Street, but amazingly she died of natural causes at a rather advanced age. I can only hope to have the same luck.

CHAPTER THREE

RIGHT AROUND THE TIME I entered high school, my father's days as a state senator in Atlanta ended and his days as an assistant district attorney in Savannah began. Though he had accomplished a lot as a senator, I feel—and I think he felt—that the ADA job was tailor-made for his personality and his talents. Dad loved all aspects of this new job. He could happily spend all day in a law library, researching case law and digging for data. He enjoyed meticulously organizing his evidence and creating his exhibits. But the real fun was waiting for him in the courtroom, where he gained a reputation as a legal dynamo. He loved the performance aspect of presenting cases to juries, and his natural flamboyance and smooth tongue ensured that their attention never wandered. I have a photo of Dad in front of a murder-case jury waving two pistols around like a Wild West outlaw, and that was typical; he always put on quite a show. Though he still suffered from periodic depression, I have no doubt that the constant activity of the ADA job helped to keep his demons at bay.

Mom seemed happy, too, one reason being that our family had moved to a two-story house in a nice, middle-class neighborhood called Magnolia Park. Mom worked full-time as a secretary in an accounting firm and enjoyed the work. She loved gardening and her rose garden flourished in those years. When muscle damage in the right side of her neck prohibited her from learning to paint with her right hand, Mom learned to paint with her left hand—and she got pretty good at it, too. No matter what changes were occurring around her, she always remained her steady, reliable self. I loved that about her then, and I love it now.

My parents enrolled me at Savannah's Benedictine Military School for several reasons. Like a lot of teenagers at the time, I had been letting my freak flag fly in public school, wearing long hair, smoking weed, and blasting rock music. They thought I needed a more disciplined and structured atmosphere. But the racial problem in the public schools was probably the biggest reason for the change of venue. I know that some reading this might think Dad was hypocritical to pull me out of there after he'd worked so hard for integration, but I don't feel that way. The man was so idealistic that I don't think he could have imagined the violence that occurred after busing began, and when it did, he was totally shocked and extremely disappointed. It's easy to judge from afar, but when it's your own child in a potentially explosive situation, things look a little different.

Benedictine was an all-male, Catholic school founded in 1902 by Benedictine monks, and the majority of its students were Irish-Catholic kids who came from large families. But there were also some Jewish kids there, most of whom came from prominent families that had resided in Savannah since the colonial days. And there were a few black kids enrolled, too; I think there were two of them on the football team with me. Anyway, race was not much of an issue at Benedictine. The headmaster, Father Aelred Beck, ran a tight ship, and cleanliness and conformity were the order of the day. I knew I should have been grateful that my parents stretched their tight budget to send me to a fine school and protect me from harm, but I rebelled immediately and things got off to a horrible start.

The very worst part about this new school was that students were required to enroll in ROTC for the first two years. This meant a buzz haircut, a military uniform, and everything spit 'n' polished at all times. I just couldn't believe that I was expected to go from this long-haired free spirit to the kind of uptight square I'd laughed at my whole life. Dad was supposed to be some big liberal! Why was he doing this to me? But my many and loud protests fell on deaf ears, and soon I was marching and drilling and absolutely hating every moment of it. The only good thing about Benedictine, I felt at the time, was that it was located in Savannah and was only a short drive from our new home in Magnolia Park. I could escape at the end of the day; just the thought of boarding at a place like that made me want to throw up.

I dreaded my classes, too. I loved reading, short stories and poetry in particular, but I wasn't about to admit that to my teachers or anyone else. "Brains" were hopelessly un-cool. Instead, I was a clown and a trouble-maker, and it seemed I was getting hauled into the headmaster's office on a weekly basis. When the teachers decided to handle me themselves, it was even worse. Head football coach Jim Walsh was also a history teacher, and if you fell asleep in his class, he'd "book you"—take a thick, heavy book and smash it right over your head. Coach Cannon, who was both the assistant football coach and the baseball coach, taught some classes, too. I don't remember which ones, but I do remember his paddle. It was a baseball bat that was cut off short and sawed in half, so that one side of it was flat. Holes had been drilled into it to better accommodate the air flow when he smacked it across your butt as you leaned over his desk. This was a punishment indeed, but I did not feel it was a punishment as humiliating (or as painful) as the one my science teacher preferred: kneeling on the hard, linoleum floor for the entire period. When I finally refused to do this, it was right back to Father Beck's office, where my distraught parents were waiting.

The older I got, the more it bothered me when teachers got on my case. I didn't see it as "just discipline." Whether it was real or only in my head, I always saw it as mockery and degradation, and I was always sure of the reason: I was the fat kid. To this day, whenever I am reprimanded or criti-cized harshly, there is a part of me that still feels that way, a part of me that will always be the fat kid. Back then, I decided that the only way to fight fire was with fire, and though I couldn't beat up my teachers, I began to beat up plenty of other people, even grown men on occasion. And I shot my mouth off constantly, wherever and whenever. I can remember my tiny Latin teacher, Father Mario, shaking his head and saying in a foreign accent I was never able to identify, "Meester Searcey, the empty can makes the most noise." I know now that he was absolutely correct, but at the time, I didn't know what the heck he meant.

At least girls were starting to pay attention to me, and my childhood innocence would soon be a thing of the past. In high school, my teammates and I started dating cheerleaders from St. Vincent's, a Catholic girls' school across town. My parents neither encouraged me nor discouraged me in this area. They left it up to my questionable discretion, and of course as a horny, heterosexual teenager, I was going to go after as many girls as I could. It was the Seventies, and… Well, it was the Seventies. Need I say more?

Aside from my schooling, Dad and Mom gave me a lot of freedom. They let me start driving at around age thirteen, partly because they just wanted someone to be their cigarette delivery boy. I was big and tall enough to pass for an adult, and I never got pulled over. A few years later, they bought me a brand-new Plymouth Barracuda with an 8-track tape player, and, boy, did I think I was something in that machine, cranking Blue Oyster Cult and Jethro Tull. Yes, it all went just fine until the night I drunkenly drove off a high embankment on the way to a beach party, totaling my beloved Barracuda. I crawled out of the wreckage none the worse for wear, and didn't see any reason why I should miss a kick-ass beach party, so I abandoned the car and went on my way, finally arriving home at about 5:30 AM. Neither the police nor my parents were too happy about this, but Dad got me out of trouble, and that was typical Savannah justice. I'll never forget when the long-time mayor, John Rousakis, who was a good friend of my father's (of course), was pulled over for DUI and blew a .10. The scandal wasn't that Rousakis was driving drunk; the scandal was that he was *actually charged* with the crime. The Dudley Moore/Bo Derek movie *10* was a big hit at the time, and the mayor's idea of damage control was to prance around town in a tee shirt that read, "I'm a Perfect .10." I'm not kidding.

Anyway, all this drama, and I *still* sucked at football! 'Til my junior year, that is. Sometimes, things all seem to fall into place in a very short period of time, and that's what happened. I was blessedly freed from ROTC that year, and Coach Walsh and fellow coach John Stephens had never given up on me, encouraging me to lose weight and push myself in practice. As I got taller and faster on my feet, the weight did come off, and my self-esteem improved dramatically as I became a stand-out defensive lineman. My teammates and I called Coach Walsh "The Cat" because he was so quick, and though he was a hard-ass, he was also a caring, ethical role model. From my team alone, he sent three guys to Georgia, one guy to Georgia Tech, one guy to Alabama, and one guy to Notre Dame. It takes a lot more than luck to do that, and I was never more proud than when, decades later, Coach Walsh introduced me when I was inducted into the Greater Savannah Athletic Hall of Fame.

My hippie friends from the old days didn't see much of me anymore, and I bonded tightly with the guys on my team. None of us could get enough football; after playing a game for Benedictine on Friday night, we'd sometimes spend all day Saturday and Sunday playing *more* football on sandlots. We worked out together; we cut lawns together, we bar-b-cued together; we jumped off bridges into the river together. There was no cell phoning, no texting, no Internet, no gaming; we actually had to go somewhere and meet other human beings in order to do stuff, and it was wonderful. Those years were some of the best of my life, and even at my lowest point, I held onto those memories to give me just a scrap of hope.

Not everyone in my life thought football was a good thing for me. My paternal grandmother was a very conservative, repressed woman who thought American football was "barbaric." In Britain, she said, sports were civilized, encouraging duty and honor rather than vanity and violence. She saw what I was doing with all these Irish-Catholic "gingers" as little more than brawling. Sadly, though my grandparents lived right across the street from us, Grandmother and I were never close, and the older I got, the more I understood why my grandfather shipped out to sea every chance he could. Still, as my senior year approached, I felt revitalized and excited, and no one—not my grandmother nor anyone else—was going to dissuade me from going for my dream.

Senior year was crazy. All of a sudden, I was a good football player—a *really* good football player. I almost couldn't believe it when I started getting all those letters and calls from universities. I had to kind of remind myself why: "You were the captain of Georgia's All-State Team. You deserve this." I won't deny that I developed a little arrogance. It's almost impossible to excel in any sport at that level if you don't. And the kind of attention I was getting… Well, I'll tell you about it and you can decide if you'd get a little arrogant, too.

Almost every weekday afternoon that Fall, when I'd walk out the front doors of Benedictine to go and eat my lunch, there would be an assistant coach from one southern university or another waiting there to talk to me and tell me how amazing I was. Sometimes there would even be *two* coaches milling around, and both of them would shout "Hey, Bill!" and follow me like a couple of puppy dogs as my classmates watched with great curiosity. Suddenly a lot of those classmates wanted to be my friends, and I highly doubt it was coincidental. When I got home in the evening, there would be phone calls from even more university coaches and assistant coaches, telling me how *their* schools were the ones that would do the most for *me*.

After every Friday-night game at Savannah's Memorial Stadium, which was always crowded with both young people and faithful Benedictine alumni, I'd drive out to the airport, where a private jet was waiting just for me. One week the jet would be from the University of South Carolina, the next week from the University of Virginia, the next week from the University of Georgia, the next week from the University of Alabama, the next week from the University of Florida, and on and on. This was back when there weren't too many of those pesky rules about recruiting, and when I got to whatever campus I was going to, I would be waited on hand and foot like a king. They'd wine me and dine me and surround me with the prettiest "co-eds" (as female students were called then) they could find. I don't want to make it sound sordid; it's not like they were hiring hookers for me or something. But they did show me a real good time, giving me a great seat at the football game on Saturday, introducing me to lots of fun people at lots of fun parties, and constantly stroking my ego. Then they'd fly me back home on Sunday night, and Monday morning I'd be back in class. There was almost something surreal about it.

South Carolina was hot and heavy for me right from the start. I flew out there and the coach, Jim Carlin, gave me a very convincing sales pitch. I liked Carlin's personality a lot, and I liked the school, too. So, I gave him a tentative yes, but with one condition. With the audacity only an endlessly-flattered kid could muster, I said, "Yeah, sure—I'll play for you next year. But don't announce it yet, okay? I want to fly out to all these other schools and party every weekend." No way was I going to give up my new, luxury, jet-setting lifestyle one second before I absolutely had to. Coach Carlin said he understood and would keep our agreement under wraps, and he did. For months after, I continued to zoom around the southeastern U.S. like some kind of mini-playboy, milking the system for all it was worth.

Predictably, the handshake agreement with Carlin and South Carolina turned into a huge fiasco. As I rolled on through Dixie, I decided I liked other schools a lot better, for lots of different reasons. I'll be honest: I almost chose Florida State simply for the hotness of its girls, which was at around the same level as that of about a thousand suns. They were gorgeous! But their team at that time was so horrible that even their beauties could not overcome common sense. Georgia was also way up there, if only because they stalked me like a deranged lover. When I'd ask Dad to help me with my decision, he'd shake his head and tell me that the choice had to be mine and mine alone. (That couldn't have been easy for him: As a Georgia alumnus he had often taken me to Athens to watch his beloved team, the "Dawgs," play.)

And then the call came one night: "Hello, this is Coach Bear Bryant."

My response? "Come on! Who is this?!" Actually, it was a little spicier than that, but you get my drift. Even with all the insane attention I'd been getting lately, I just couldn't believe it. It was like God calling on the phone; it just doesn't happen.

"No, really. It's Coach Bryant."

"Who is this, man? I'm going to hang up." Again, I sprinkled this statement with a few words I won't repeat here.

When he finally, after about five minutes, convinced me of who he was, I apologized profusely for my disbelief and the obscenities. But Coach Bryant didn't even seem offended, and after a brief chat, he said the magic words that sealed my fate: "We're playing So-and-So this week, and I really wish you were on our team right now."

Big deal, right? I mean, a zillion other coaches and assistant coaches had said the same thing to me in the last six months or so. But hearing those words come out of "Bear" Bryant, the greatest college football coach ever, was a whole different thing, and my mind was made up immediately.

"I want to come play for you next year," I said, "but I had this verbal agreement with South Carolina. Please don't announce it to the press until I call Jim Carlin, okay?"

Well, he said okay, but the next morning it was all over the sports pages and I was getting frantic calls from South Carolina. It wasn't pleasant, and I felt guilty. But all that was forgotten by the time Coach Bryant came to

Savannah to personally sign me on Signing Day, which was a great honor that got me tons of press. I picked him up at the airport, and though I'd met him once before with my parents, it was kind of intimidating—okay, really intimidating—being alone with him in my car. He didn't say much, just sat there chain-smoking and mercilessly crushing the butts in my ashtray.

Yep, I was sweating bullets. But I was on my way.

CHAPTER FOUR

PAUL "BEAR" BRYANT, the most powerful and influential man to ever coach college football, was once approached by a guest at a victory party who told him, "Coach, your shirt has a hole in it."

"Yeah, I know," Bryant replied. "I always tear a small hole in my tee shirts so I'll never forget where I came from."

Where he came from was Moro Bottom, Arkansas, the eleventh of twelve children born to Monroe and Ida Bryant. Raised in four-room shack with no electricity or running water, he had managed to claw his way out of grinding poverty to win a scholarship to play football at the University of Alabama, then went on to head coaching jobs at the University of Maryland, the University of Kentucky, Texas A&M, and of course, Alabama. Out of almost nothing, he built himself into a legend. My new coach was the last guy in the world who was going to accept any excuses from me or anyone else. But as tough as he could be, he was also a self-described "mama's boy." One of the first things he said to us incoming freshmen in the fall of 1976 was, "I want each of you boys to write a letter to your mama every week."

I was so excited and happy to get to Tuscaloosa. Sure, Savannah was home, and I missed it sometimes, but not really enough to call it "home-sickness." The heart of the campus at Alabama was The Quad, with its historical buildings that had been built to replace those that were destroyed in the Civil War. A beautiful lawn and mature trees swept out to the administrative buildings, and beyond those were the huge, two-story, white mansions that housed Alabama's many fraternities and sororities. Alabama is a very Greek-oriented university, but we football players were too busy with our ultra-manly pursuits to worry about silly little pledge pins. The frat boys would drunkenly cheer for us every game day, and after every game, we would drunkenly crash their parties, but that was the extent of it. Neither side was really "feeling the love."

Our alternative to the frat house was Bryant Hall, opened in 1965 and named after Coach Bryant, of course. The rooms at Bryant Hall were your typical dorm rooms, two beds and two desks. Nothing remarkable about the accommodations themselves, but as Allen Barra noted in his book *The Last Coach: The Life of Paul "Bear" Bryant,* "no one did more to accelerate the trend toward isolating football players from mainstream university life. Bryant was one of the first coaches to insist that his players sleep and eat entirely apart from the student body, and he was absolutely adamant in rejecting the label of 'student-athletes,' created and approved by the National Collegiate Athletic Association (NCAA). 'My players,' he insisted on numerous occasions, 'are athletes first and students second.'" Barra goes on to point out the lack of hypocrisy in this statement, and who could disagree? It's not even an opinion; it's simply a fact. When I was at Alabama, I didn't think badly of those who didn't play football, because I didn't even think of them at all. There was very, very little contact.

My first roommate at Bryant Hall, Doug Something-or-Other, was quite a piece of work. We would now call his condition "OCD," I guess, but back then, no one knew what it was. He was constantly cleaning, cleaning, cleaning—and getting all over my case because I didn't do the same. When Doug went to take a shower, he'd have to break down and touch the doorknob with a sleeve-covered hand to get out of our room, but he'd leave the door open a crack so that when he came back, he could just nudge it open with his big toe. Well, I'd close the door on him just to watch him throw a fit. I'd also take every opportunity to mess up his bed and his desktop. I know it was mean, but he was driving me nuts and I just wanted him out of there. I soon accomplished my mission and had the room to myself for the rest of the school year, but still I wondered: How the hell does a guy with this problem play the messiest sport there is?

I had no idea what to major in. Honestly, I just didn't care. I didn't want to be an attorney like my dad; I didn't want to be a teacher… Heck, I didn't even want to be a coach. The only thing I cared about was *playing* football, and to play football I had to pass 24 hours of classes a year. I decided I was going to do the absolute bare minimum, ignoring academics altogether during football season, picking up 12 hours in the spring and then another 12 hours in the summer. Naturally, I put forth zero effort and took the easiest classes I could find, but sometimes karma came back to bite me, like when I took a course called "Wilderness Education."

"Wilderness Education" was okay up until the final exam, which was a night spent alone in the Talladega National Forest with nothing but a container of water. I had injured myself at practice and was on crutches, but the professor, a disturbed Viet Nam veteran, didn't think that was any excuse. He personally drove me deep into the forest, stopped at the end of a dirt road, snarled "Get out!", and abandoned me until the next morning. I sat with my back to a tree all night in the sweltering heat, just waiting for a snake or a bobcat to come and kill me. Hearing intermittent gunshots didn't exactly calm the nightmarish, *Deliverance*-y thoughts that were going through my head. I was only surprised that I didn't hear a banjo, too.

My grades weren't bad; they were nonexistent. There wasn't a whole lot of pressure from Coach Bryant about grades, because he had "people" who were watching your academic progress (or non-progress) and keeping him informed. You weren't called into his office unless the situation was totally out of control, and the office was set up to let you know that you'd better get a grip, and fast. It was like Mr. Potter's office in *It's a Wonderful Life*: a huge, high desk for him, and across from it, a sofa in which you would sink lower and lower and lower, so that by the end of your visit, you felt totally enveloped in the thing.

But once when I was really screwing up, Coach Bryant actually came looking for me. It was yet another blistering-hot, summer morning, and I was passed out in bed, buck naked and hung over from the previous night's partying. The doors in Bryant Hall were very heavy, and suddenly someone was pounding the living crap out of mine. I awoke with a start, and after taking a few seconds to orient myself, I started yelling, "If I have to get up and answer that door, I'm gonna whip your butt!" But the banging continued. And continued. "I'm gettin' up, and if you're not gone, you're gettin' a beat down!"

As soon as I opened the door and saw the shoes, I knew who it was. I didn't even want to look up at the face, but of course I did—right about the time I realized that I'd forgotten to throw on a robe. Yes, I was standing there as naked as the day I was born, in front of Coach Paul "Bear" Bryant.

"What a thing to see without a gun," Coach said with a grimace. "Aren't you supposed to be in class, boy?"

"Yes, sir."

"You get to class, and when you're through, you come see me at the coliseum."

"Yes, sir."

I ran laps around that practice field for what seemed like an eternity that day before he let me go. But at least by that time, I was used to it. My first few practices at Alabama, on the other hand, can only be described with one word: hell. Absolute hell. Never before or since have I pushed my body to such extremes, and there were times when I wondered how I kept going, but I did. I had to, because I wasn't the big star anymore. All-American? Big deal! *Everyone* there was an All-American. I was suddenly surrounded by hundreds of guys who were just as good as I was, and it was a rude awakening. But I made up my mind that I was going to do whatever I had to do so that I could once again be a stand-out player.

The equipment at Alabama was nothing special; in fact, it would look downright primitive to today's college players. Coach Bryant was so old school. He didn't think you needed much more than guts, a track to run laps on, and a few wooden benches. I have to wonder what he'd think of the locker room at Alabama today, with its flat-screen TVs and its smoothie bar. In my day, the locker room was as Spartan as it gets, and the equipment manager, Willie Meadows, a tough old coot with a chip on his shoulder the size of Coosa County, thought freshman were the lowest form of life on earth.

"Good morning," you'd say, as you cautiously approached the equipment room.

"What's so good about it?" he'd snap, as he threw an ill-fitting jersey, a mismatched pair of socks, and a jock strap with absolutely no elasticity left in it at your head. "Now, get the hell out of here!" That Willie, always a kind word. But I learned fast that complaining was not the answer; he'd just make it even tougher on you if you complained.

Weight-training routines were almost nonexistent when I was at Alabama, but I had worked out in Savannah with older guys for years, so I devised my own routines in my college years. And was I glad I did. I really felt it gave me an edge, especially since I was a lineman. Cardio is great, but in my role, I needed that strength training, too. Coach Bryant, though, like of lot of older coaches back then, saw it as "fancy"—scientific baloney that was being pushed on athletes by city-slicker experts. So my official training continued to be endless, brutal cardio.

Okay, it wasn't "endless." Workouts usually lasted about an hour and a half. But "brutal"? Definitely. In winter training, the toughest training of the year, it was constant movement: running laps, calisthenics, jumping rope, agility drills, running stadium steps. There were times when I projectile vomited into one of the plastic-lined, 55-gallon drums that were put there just for puking purposes. There were times when I needed to be held up by my teammates on the way back to the locker room. There were times when I needed to sit on a metal chair in the shower, because my legs were shaking too badly to stand up. No shame in any of that, though; it meant I was doing what I was supposed to do. And at least winter training had a silver lining: The unbearable heat was not torturing you as you went about your business.

Did I say "business"? Yeah, I did see it as a job, even though we of course were not paid for our work. And that's just how some of the "bosses" under Coach Bryant expected you to see it. Dee Powell, the offensive line coach, was one of the famous "Junction Boys" who had played for Bryant at Texas A&M, and when I say he was hardcore, I mean he was hardcore. He'd get out there on the field and demonstrate exactly what he wanted us to do, and if it meant butting heads while wearing no helmet and leaving practice with blood running out of his ears and down his shirt, well, it was all in a day's work. Dude Hennessy, described by one sportswriter as "the coaching staff's cheerleader, its funnybone, its alter ego, its blithe spririt," was a short guy, but he could blithely kick your butt if you got out of line. Jack Rutledge, an offensive line and special teams coach who lived in an apartment in Bryant Hall with his wife and kids, kept a constant eye on us and had the unenviable job of enforcing curfew.

And then there was Ken Donahue, the ex-Marine turned defensive coordinator. Now, some hard-core coaches don't care if you party off the field, as long as you show up and win. That wasn't the case with Coach Donahue. He didn't drink, didn't smoke, didn't cuss—and if he caught *you* doing any of those things, you were in trouble. One weekend, I was supposed to show a recruit around campus, but I didn't have a car, so Coach Donahue lent me his car. Needless to say, it was a bad decision on his part, but I guess he thought his stern warning was enough: "No drinking in this car. I'd better not find out you were drinking."

Naturally the recruit wanted to party, and so did I, and I accidentally left an empty liquor bottle under the front seat of Donahue's car. It might not have been so bad if his pastor had not been in the car with him the next day when he slammed on the brakes and that bottle came rolling out from under the seat, but he was, and I was forced to "run extra" every day after practice for the rest of the year. But I've got to hand it to Coach Donahue: He might have been an uptight, nervous guy, but he worked harder than anyone, and though he was in his mid-fifties at the time, he could outrun any of the young men he was coaching. He turned a lot of guys into great players, and sent a lot of his protégés to the NFL.

Over the five years I played at Alabama, I met a variety of personalities. Quarterback Don Jacobs was my roommate for a year, and we had a good relationship. Don really didn't look much like a football player. He was a skinny, scrawny, good ol' country boy who always had a mouth full of chewing tobacco. Another quarterback, Steadman Shealy, who went on to become an attorney, was probably the most mature, stable player in my class, and there was no tobacco—or booze, for that matter—involved for Steadman. He was a devout Christian. I respected him because he was a great leader and an excellent student, but when it came to socializing, he was not the type I gravitated toward.

We all bonded over football, but during our off time, I wanted to run with fellow bad boys. One of those bad boys was the funniest guy on the team, an incorrigible prankster who seemed to have an endless supply of fireworks and shaving cream. Along with him and about five others, I would hang out in the little dive bars of Tuscaloosa, getting loaded and chasing girls. One night, when we were scheduled to play LSU in Birmingham the next day, the "usual suspects" and I were caught in a hotel room playing poker after curfew by trainer Jim "Goose" Goosetree. I screamed "Goosetree!" and everyone scattered, though it was pointless because we were trapped. A teammate and I were found cowering in the bathroom. Goose took down all our names, but promised to withhold the information if we won the next game.

"Thanks, Goose," I said. "If you'd said something to Coach Bryant, we'd probably be on the bus home right now."

"Bus, hell!" Goose replied. "You'd be *walking* home right now." Looking at his watch, he added, "You'd be at the Abernant and Bucksville exit right about now!"

Goose always knew everything about our shenanigans, and he was very close to Coach Bryant, so he wielded a lot of power. He was really the only one who could keep you out of practice if you were hurt; if Goose said it was okay, it was okay. And if he thought you were "letting yourself go," watch out. After summer break one year, a player came back a few pounds heavier. "Boy, whatchoo been doin' all summer, son?" Goose asked him in his funny little southern drawl.

"Just workin' out, Coach," the player replied.

"Hell, looks like someone stuck an air hose up your butt."

One of the nicest things about life at Alabama, after all I'd witnessed in Savannah, was the lack of racial tension. It was pretty amazing, because just a decade or so earlier, Coach Bryant was being roundly criticized for his supposed friendship with Alabama's rabidly segregationist governor, George Wallace. But in truth, Bryant hated Wallace's racist policy, and resented that he was missing out on some of the best recruitment opportunities because of it. He worked hard behind the scenes to integrate the U of A, and by the time I got there, it didn't seem like much of an issue at all. I and other white players went to lots of black fraternity and sorority parties, and I never saw any racially-motivated altercations. Not that there wasn't plenty of brawling, but booze was the only culprit, as far as I could see.

Coach Bryant made it clear that nothing—neither racism nor anything else—would be allowed to get in the way of his unrelenting and sometimes even irrational coaching methods. What do I mean by "irrational"? Well, like the time he made us do a 6:00 AM, Sunday morning practice because we'd *won* a game, 35-0, but not the *way* he wanted us to win it.

Finally, at 8:00 AM, he blew the whistle and we all gathered around him. "Okay, all you Christian boys go shower and get to church. The rest of you stay with me and we're gonna practice some more." We were, of course, all Christian boys that day, even me. For the first time in my life, I claimed Christianity, but it would be a long, long time before actually embraced it.

CHAPTER FIVE

I N 1977, my sophomore year at Alabama, I was "redshirted," which meant I could practice with the team but could not play in games. Redshirting is a practice that has been going on in college football since 1937, when the University of Nebraska sat out Warren Alfson for a year. Simply put, it is a way to lengthen a player's eligibility from four years to five years. There are many reasons a team might redshirt a player: to allow for the final years of his physical growth, to allow him to learn a complex playbook, to accommodate a medical problem or injury, etc. And I sure wasn't happy when I heard the reason my coaches had decided to redshirt me: They were moving me from defense to offense.

It seemed like I'd been playing defense forever, and it was just second nature to me. I saw this switch as throwing away all the training and hard work I'd done since I was a kid. It was a very tough transition. At one point that season, I just up and left—hitchhiked to Atlanta and thought, "Screw it. It's over." Coach Bryant was furious, but he still convinced me to change my mind ("Where you gonna go? You ain't got nowhere to go.") A part of me was hoping that if I put up enough of a fuss, they'd let me remain a defensive player. Finally, I realized that I could kick and scream about it all I wanted to, but it was going to happen regardless. Gradually, I changed my attitude and by the end of my redshirt year, I was raring to go. I felt strong and positive as an offensive lineman, and I realized that my coaches had made the right decision.

The first big game I played in during my junior year in 1978 was the Nebraska game, which was played at Legion Field in Birmingham. It's hard to describe the electric feeling we experienced before a game like that. Our names might not have been household names throughout the land, but where we were, we were *stars*. The night before a game at Legion Field, we'd stay in a hotel outside the city in a little town called Bessemer. On Saturday morning, we'd pile into buses to be escorted by state troopers all the way from Bessemer to the field. It was like a parade; thousands of people would line the streets, clapping and cheering, hanging out of the windows of their homes and cars. And over at Legion Field, the hardcore fans were way ahead of us; many had started their tailgating on Tuesday or Wednesday!

I began as a starter that year, but it seemed I was always getting temporarily demoted for my off-field antics: drinking, curfew violations, bar fights. One time, I got a little too close to someone else's girlfriend at a popular Tuscaloosa bar called Down the Hatch, and he responded by grabbing a steak knife off the bar (the bartender had been cutting fruit with it) and threatening me. I grabbed him, laid him out across the bar, pulled my own knife out of my pocket, and put it right up to his neck. I wasn't going to cut him; I was just messing with him. But needless to say, first thing the next morning, my hangover and I were called into Coach Bryant's office. Again.

"Did you pull a knife on somebody last night?" He was hot boxing the Chesterfields, as usual, and I was feeling more nauseated by the second as I tried to see him through the wall of smoke.

"Yes, sir."

"Boy, you need to join the Marines. Maybe *they* can teach you some discipline."

"The Marines? Uh…"

"What is wrong with you? Where is that knife?"

"It's in my pocket."

"Give me that damn knife." I handed it over as he went on: "Boy, you could go bear huntin' with a switch—why would you carry a knife?"

"Well, I don't really have a reason. I just had it in my pocket."

"Tell me what happened."

"Well, he started it…"

After asking me to swear my story was true, Coach told me that he had heard quite a different story from my barroom foe. I was punished with the usual extra running and temporarily demoted from starter, but the other guy didn't get off the hook, either. I later heard that Bryant called him back into his office and really reamed him out but good: "Don't ever come to me and tell me a story about one of my players and not tell me the *whole* story. It'll be a sad day for you." Months later, during spring training, I saw Mr. Bar Fight at the very same bar, but he didn't recognize me because we were allowed to grow facial hair in the off-season and I looked like a cross between Grizzly Adams and Kris Kristofferson.

"There's that guy who pulled a knife on me," I said to a friend. "I'm gonna get 'im." My buddy pleaded with me to refrain, as I happened to be on crutches at the time, but I went up to the guy and said, "Do you remember me?" When he indicated the negative, I punched him the face and dropped him.

The closure was nice, but I was called into Coach Bryant's office about a zillion times more before my college career was over. Sometimes I couldn't even figure out why I was there. Once I went in and sat on that aggravating couch for what seemed like an eternity while he smoked, paced, shuffled papers, and stared into space.

Finally, he turned to me and said, "What do you want?"

"You called me in here, didn't you?"

"Ah, yeah—I can't remember what I wanted you for."

I shook my head and threw up my hands in exasperation. "What have I done?"

He looked me in the eye. "Exactly: What *have* you done?"

"I'm practicing. I'm working hard."

"Boy, all you're doing is what you're *supposed* to do. I gave you a scholarship to do those things. But what else have you done?"

Coach never specified what he wanted me to do, and I don't think he even had anything specific in mind. I believe he was trying to tell me to look inside myself to find the answers and the strength to act on them. One thing that made Coach Bryant unique was the way he treated every individual player differently, psychologically speaking, and he knew that I was a natural-born rebel. He did his best to turn that rebellion into a positive rather than a negative trait, but through no fault of his, results were mixed.

1978 was a dream season. We only lost one game, to USC. One of my favorite memories of Coach Bryant is of right before that game. We played Southern Cal in Birmingham, and I was sitting in front of my locker, which was right next to the door that led to the field. Coach was standing next to the door, wearing his trademark houndstooth fedora and slapping a rolled-up piece of paper against his hand. A ref came and knocked at the door, and when Coach opened it, the ref said, "Coach, we gotta wait five more minutes for TV."

Coach grimaced and exclaimed, "Damn it, Tom, my boys are ready to go!"

"Sorry, Coach—can't let y'all out yet. ABC wants you to hold up."

Coach closed the door and started grumbling and cursing under his breath. Five minutes later, another knock came at the door. Coach tapped me on the head with that piece of rolled-up paper and said, "Watch this, boy."

"All right, Coach," the ref told him. "ABC is ready for you to come out now."

Coach gave him a big smile. "You tell ABC that Coach Bryant says he needs five more minutes." He closed the door and looked down at me. "How do you like that, boy? That's power, right there."

It was because of that power that Coach Bryant didn't even have to *try* to pretend he was happy about some of the changes that were happening in the sports media. He didn't trust reporters anyway, and kept them away from his players as much as he possibly could. I'm glad he did, because with the mouth I had on me back then… Well, I don't even want to think about what I might have said. So, he was already wary of male reporters, but *female?* On the *field?* He was no woman hater, but he saw any kind of big change as something that would just distract him and his players. And it's hard for us to remember just how shocking the idea of a woman sports reporter was back in the 1970s; we don't even think anything of it these days when we see an attractive, knowledgeable woman like Pam Oliver or Bonnie Bernstein interviewing coaches and players. There's a famous video on Youtube of Coach Bryant reading the riot act to reporter Anne Simon, but the truth is, she just picked a really, really bad time to interview him: at halftime, when we were losing to Auburn 14-13. He had yelled at a whole lot of male reporters before, but he probably never called them afterward to apologize, as he did to Simon the next week. There were no hard feelings on either side.

In '78, we finished the regular season 10-1-0 and won the Southeastern Conference Championship. Ranked #2 in the country, we went on to beat the #1 ranked Penn State Nittany Lions 14-7 in the Sugar Bowl on January 1, 1979, our defense thrilling football fans with the famous Goal Line Stand. The Sugar Bowl was just pure fun, because by the time we rolled into New Orleans, about five days before the game, we were totally up for the challenge. We checked into a fancy hotel and were able to just relax in those days before the game. The per diem we were given might not sound like much today—a few hundred bucks—but it seemed like a lot to us, and we made the most of it, partying on Bourbon Street and attending various Bowl functions with coaches Bryant and Paterno. Then we won the big game and returned home heroes. What more could you ask for?

It was great to be a part of this kind of group triumph, but there was also a wonderful personal reward for my role in the '78 season: Henceforth, I would not only be a player, not only a part-time starter, but a letterman. *A letterman at the University of Alabama.* I was standing just below the pinnacle of college athletics, but in order reach that pinnacle, I'd have to wallow in some rather low places. You see, these were the waning days of initiation—what is now called "hazing"—into the Lettermen's Club. In fact, the year I was initiated was the very last year it was allowed on the Alabama campus. It was a week-long event. The first day, all the members of our group were required to put on a rather ridiculous uniform: overalls with nothing but a jockstrap underneath, tennis shoes with no socks, and a goofy hat. We were told we'd have to wear these same clothes all week long. Now, that part didn't seem all that bad to us because, let's face it, lots of college-aged dudes are kind of gross anyway. But that was hardly the end of it: The Pit awaited us.

The Pit was a big hole behind Bryant Hall that would fill up with rainwater, and our tormentors had been experimenting in it with their own secret recipe of garbage, rotten produce, and God knows what else. It was a filthy, reeking hellhole. We were ordered to dive into this foul mess, one at a time, and blow bubbles as we swam through it. It was disgusting, but even more disgusting was that we were not allowed to shower or change afterward. Those were our bodies and those were our clothes—for the next week. During that week, we were subjected to all kinds of humiliations: doing demeaning chores for our overlords, being forced to get down on the sidewalk on all fours and blow dust out of the cracks, enduring vicious verbal abuse.

One night the lettermen drove us all out to Lake Tuscaloosa, miles and miles from the campus. They forced us to remove our overalls so that we were wearing nothing but jockstraps and tennis shoes, and left us there, telling us we had to be back on campus by such-and-such a time. After walking for miles on a dark country road, we finally saw a light coming from a trailer park. I turned to Warren Lyles, a black kid from Birmingham, and said, "Warren, go up to one of those doors and knock and ask for help."

"Real funny, Searcey," he replied. "Black guy in nothing but a jock strap. Man, they'd lynch me." Finally, we got a ride back to campus in the back of a pick-up truck, and soon after we were made lettermen.

To say I was on top of the world in the summer of 1979 would be an understatement. I was a letterman on the National Championship team. My parents and the folks back home in Savannah were so proud. In Tuscaloosa, I was treated like a demigod. Everyone liked me. Everyone wanted to be my friend. Everyone told me that this was just the beginning; surely a fabulous NFL career was in my future. I was leading a charmed life and I was loving it. I felt invincible.

That feeling of invincibility came to a crashing end one day when I went out waterskiing with friends on Lake Tuscaloosa. We'd been drinking, of course. Heavily, of course. I was probably in the best shape of my life, but that didn't mean a thing when my ski twisted under me and excruciating pain shot through my lower leg. It hurt like crazy and I knew deep down that something was really wrong, but I didn't want to end my party day. We kept riding around in the boat and boozing, and by the time I got back to Bryant Hall, I was a mess. Elevation didn't help, ice didn't help, and the swelling was out of control. I knew I had to go to the emergency room.

After two sets of x-rays, it was determined that I had a broken ankle. I was rushed into surgery right away, where they filled me with a bunch of pins and plates that are there to this day. When I woke up, Coach Bryant was hovering in my hospital room. He was not angry or rude, but I could see in his expression how disappointed he was that I would have taken that kind of reckless chance. I was devastated. I think it was the first time in my life that I recognized a pattern of self-sabotage that had the potential to completely destroy me, and it was frightening. The doctors, both from the hospital and from our team, came in and we had a very serious consultation. Surgery back then just wasn't as sophisticated and effective as it is today, and there was only so much they'd been able to do. They told me I'd be out for the entire year—at least.

Well, I was having none of it. I was absolutely determined to play in the '79 season. In my old-fashioned plaster cast, I would go to the old-fashioned training room every day and get on an old-fashioned stationary bike and ride and ride and ride. Sometimes 20 miles. Sometimes 30 miles. Needless to say, I was not supposed to be doing that, but when I went back to the doctors in two weeks, they told me, "This is healing a lot faster than we thought it would." They were clueless and I was going to keep them clueless. I kept riding that crappy old bike and lifting crappy old weights and dreaming about another glorious season. That's what all my teammates were dreaming about, too. Our goal was back-to-back championships, and nothing was going to get in our way.

In late summer, the cast came off and I started practicing, but my ankle was real bad. Training was not a science back then. If it hurt, you put ice on it—period. I kept trying to *will* myself better, and became frustrated and angry when I just couldn't do it. It was another great year for the Crimson Tide: We went undefeated in the regular season and we went to the Sugar Bowl again and again emerged victorious, beating Arkansas 24-9. Of course I was happy about all that, but I felt I could have contributed so much more had I been in top form. I kept telling myself that all that mattered was the team, all that mattered was the championship, but my pride had taken a battering and it was hard to get my mind into a better place.

And while it was true that I was not satisfied with myself in the '79 season, even if I hadn't been injured, and even if I had played my best season ever, I probably still wouldn't have been satisfied with myself. Why? Because that's what we were taught in the Alabama football program: Never be satisfied. Even if you're winning, you can always win better. Coach Bryant would say, "Always practice and play as though you're losing." I truly felt I'd done that after the waterskiing accident. I'd pushed myself to the absolute limit in '79, even though the personal outcome had not been what I wanted. And that's why I was so confused and upset about what happened in '80.

CHAPTER SIX

THINGS COULDN'T HAVE LOOKED BETTER as we went into the 1980 season. We had won the national championships of 1978 and 1979. Bear Bryant had now led the University of Alabama to as many national titles—six—as had been won by the only other college coach who shared his legendary status, Notre Dame's Knute Rockne. The Crimson Tide was now not just another college football team, but a fabled institution that had worked its way into the American psyche as a symbol of pride and victory.

When we players turned on our transistor radios (don't laugh, kids), we heard Steely Dan's hit song *Deacon Blues* wafting through the hot, humid air: *"They call Alabama the Crimson Tide..."* Indeed, that song was all about how even those fans who rooted for other teams had to grudgingly admit that we were the best. Donald Fagan said that when he first sang that line to his songwriting partner, Walter Becker, a Wake Forest Demon Deacons fan, Becker said, "You mean it's like, they call these cracker ass***** this grandiose name like the Crimson Tide, and I'm this loser, so they call me this other grandiose name, Deacon Blues?" When Fagan replied, "Yeah," Becker said, "Cool! Let's finish it!"

Not only the institution but its leader had become a pop culture icon. Coach Bryant was doing things like appearing on a Bob Hope TV special

39

with former Alabama quarterback and NFL great Joe Namath. Search for it on Youtube if you're interested in seeing the very best and the very worst of the Seventies all rolled into one neat, seven-minute package. Coach somehow seems relaxed *and* wooden at the same time, while the always-game Namath and the old pro Hope do what they can to help him out. Between the time it was taped and the time it aired, Iranian militants took over the American Embassy in Tehran and held 52 Americans hostage, so some cultural references, like "Billy Carter," stayed in, while others, like "the Ayatollah," had to be edited. Within seconds, the viewer is wondering, "Who on earth asked Bear Bryant to cut off a kicker's foot? And why?" It's all chopped up.

So, some of us were really famous and some of us were kind of famous, but all of us expected big things out of the 1980 season. I had rededicated myself to the program, practicing and working out like a man possessed and staying out of trouble. That's why I was so shocked when, in the spring of my junior year, Coach Bryant called me into his office and said, "Bill, I've decided to take your scholarship away from you."

I was devastated, of course. "Why?"

"I just feel it's the best thing for the team. If you want to come back as a walk-on next season you can stay at Bryant Hall this summer, but I'm sure you won't want to do that."

"I don't know." I could barely get the words out of my mouth, I was so stunned. "I'll let you know."

I went back to my room and called my mother, hoping for some coddling. I didn't get it. "Well, you can't come home. You don't have a place to come home to." This response was so unlike Mom. I don't know if she was playing some kind of mind game to get my scholarship back, or what. But she sure turned me right around, and I immediately went back to Coach's office and told him, "I'll be back in August." He cracked a sly smile but said nothing.

The first day back, I was at the bottom of the bottom, but within two weeks, I had moved through the scout team, the third team, the second team, and finally got myself back onto the first team. But boy, did they make me work for it. They drove me harder than they ever had, never letting me come out of practice, even to take a water break. And it got right down to the wire; with school starting the next week, I still didn't have any confirmation that I was back on the team.

Then I heard Coach Bryant's golf cart coming up behind me as I walked off the field. "Bill!" I turned around and watched him get out of the cart and extend his hand. "Congratulations, son. You got your scholarship back." That was one of the most marvelous moments of my life, and I knew I'd earned it.

Unfortunately, the Eighties were just not going to live up to the glory and hype of the Seventies, and 1980 tuned out to be a disappointment. When we lost our first game to Mississippi State (6-3) since 1957, it ended Alabama's all-time school record of 28 wins in a row. Though we only gave up 98 points the whole season, Ole Miss scored 35 of those points! They really took a chunk out of us, and we also lost to Notre Dame that season, 7-0. For the first time since '76, we failed to win the SEC championship. We did win the 1981 Cotton Bowl against Baylor, but I'd be lying if I told you it didn't feel like a letdown. I had wanted—as all athletes want—to go out on a high note. But of course, I wasn't "going out" forever; though no one else expected me to have a pro career at that point, I wasn't giving up on that goal, so the 1980 season wasn't like the greatest tragedy of my life or something. Just disappointing.

Yes, it was time for me to go out into "the real world," and not until I got there would I realize that even though we Alabama players were some of the toughest guys in America, we had also lived in a strange kind of protective cocoon. Between the Tuscaloosa legal authorities, the campus police, the school officials, the coaching staff, the local business owners, and just average everyday citizens, there seemed to be a crazy, underground phone network that traced our movements, gauged our partying levels, and attempted to mitigate any potentially disastrous situations. If the university had any official rules about drinking and partying, I never knew what they were. If they ever enforced them, I don't remember it. As long as we weren't damaging property or physically harming someone, they'd just break us up and shoo us away. The Tuscaloosa police were about keeping the peace, not about arresting a bunch of people. They knew we were just a bunch of young, drunken idiots.

And, boy, was I a young, drunken idiot on the day I got arrested for

DUI. It was right after my freshman year, and it happened—thank goodness—in Georgia rather than Alabama. With my girlfriend at the time and a buddy of mine, I was headed to see some friends who played football for Georgia, and I was driving my father-assigned college car, a white Ford Grenada with a lovely puke-green interior and matching puke-green top. Dad was "so over" trying to please me when it came to cars. No more sexy, macho cars for me. Just a piece of crap like most college students drive. Anyway, my friends pooled their resources and bailed me out of jail, I paid a fine of about $140, and the DUI is not on my record because my father was state senator William Searcey. I sometimes wonder what would have happened if I'd been busted in Alabama rather than Georgia. I probably would have been escorted back to our dorm without a citation being issued, but that doesn't mean I would not have gotten in trouble. Coach Bryant would have found out, and made me wish I was behind bars instead of in his office.

Drugs? Yeah, even in college, I was doing plenty of stuff I wasn't supposed be doing. Everybody knows—and has known for what seems like forever—that I've used drugs. As for fellow players and students? Yes, Alabama is a party school, and yes, it was the freewheeling Seventies, but believe me, there were lots of kids back then who wouldn't have even known where to buy drugs if they'd wanted them. And lots who just had no interest at all. Apparently, some of them were at U. of A. to actually *study*.

I never heard of anyone, jock or not, getting arrested for drugs during my college days. I really don't know if the cops would have busted one of "us," but if they had and Coach Bryant had found out about it, I have no doubt that it would have meant banishment from the team. Sure, Coach had his own vices. He smoked like a chimney and drank—a lot. But in those days, we had what was called the "Generation Gap." Oldsters who were killing themselves with alcohol and tobacco thought that marijuana was something one could "overdose" on, and that one could get "hooked" on LSD the same way you could on cocaine. They didn't understand illegal drugs and they didn't *want* to understand them. If it was illegal, then it must be worse than the legal drugs—period. I don't know why I wasn't more worried about getting busted for drugs at the time. Just because worrying wasn't really my thing, I guess. I was too young and too crazy for worry. I'd just go into Birmingham, get a bag of weed, and get high. And when I didn't have weed, I sure wasn't going through any withdrawals or shakes or any of the other stuff the dumb adults warned us about. I was fine and dandy either way.

Another thing neither I nor any of my teammates ever worried about was political correctness. The Crimson Tide had been integrated and everyone seemed to be getting along just fine, so what more was there to do? No one blinked an eye when one of the frats held their annual "Indian Party," and we jocks were happy to join in, attaching feathers to our hair and painting our faces with "war paint." Actually, our dorm coach Jack Rutledge *did* blink an eye, but not because we were doing this bad impersonation of Native Americans. We were just late getting back to Bryant Hall that night, that's all, and we whooped and hollered as we rampaged up the stairwell and met Coach Rutledge at the top of the stairs. "Get to your damn rooms, right now!" Oh, that poor man and his poor wife. The stories they could tell about trying to raise a family in that place! I still feel so much love for them.

Like most college athletes in any age, I had a good dating life. And like at any other university, some female students at Alabama put great store in dating athletes, while others just didn't think it was a big deal. It shocks me when I hear news stories about the problem of date rape on college campuses today, because I didn't see any of that, and I knew and hung out with some pretty wild guys. That kind of thing never seemed to enter their minds. I didn't hear them talk about it, and I didn't see them do it. As for me, I tried to keep dating friendly and polite rather than serious and heavy. I was not ready for commitment, so I didn't want to make any promises I couldn't keep.

It all seemed a lot more innocent and natural than what goes on these days. Sure, there might have been a few *Playboys* or *Penthouses* lying around someone's dorm room, but we weren't living in a world saturated with porn, like young people are today. As the father of a teenage boy, I know what goes on now, with kids sexting and sending naked photos of themselves to one another. Heck, the Brett Favre scandal showed that even adults in professional sports, who should know better, are doing it. It doesn't surprise me, I guess, that the guys are into it, but the girls... Well, it's like they've just given up and given in. That's what I don't get.

Of course, cell phone cameras can be used to capture all kinds of bad behavior, not just sex, and I am so grateful that they weren't around in the Seventies. Jeez, Coach wouldn't even allow us to talk to the relatively harmless local press without getting top-secret, highest-level permission; can you imagine what his reaction to social media would have been? His head would have exploded. And can you imagine what some of my tweets would have been like?

"Think I just broke my leg, but I'm gonna keep partying, yo! Woo-hoo!"

"Had to pull out my knife at Down the Hatch. That ain't right, man. : ("

"Coach just saw me naked cuz I forgot to put a robe on! LOL!!!"

So, yeah… It's a *really* good thing that that kind of technology was not at my fingertips.

Coach Bryant discouraged any behavior that was detrimental to the football team, but also behavior that would be detrimental in our lives later on. He was always talking about doing the right things, being good citizens, and behaving in a mature fashion. Being young, we didn't always listen. We couldn't imagine ourselves inhabiting middle-aged bodies and doing boring stuff like raising kids. Living amongst ourselves, eating amongst ourselves, working out amongst ourselves, partying amongst ourselves… That isolation shined a bright light on us and made us feel that we would always be young, invincible stars. So, the semi-quarantine imposed on us by Coach Bryant, the same thing that worked miracles on the football field and turned us into the most ferocious college athletics team in the nation, did have some unintended consequences, I think. But the bottom line is, we were grown adults, and it was up to us to make something of our lives when our days at the University of Alabama came to an end.

CHAPTER SEVEN

How ironic that I should hear about the death of Ben Davidson, the Oakland Raiders lineman and actor, just as I begin to write about my transition from college to the pros. In the late Sixties, Davidson and Raiders coach Al Davis created a renegade team that was the meanest, toughest, and roughest in the business, and all through the Seventies they inspired wild youngsters like me. It was all about fame and fortune, doing it your own way and not worrying too much about using other people as stepping stones. About two years before he died, Ben Davidson told the *Los Angeles Times*, "I'm 70 years old and I've never had a real job." Sports, Hollywood, beer commercials, motorcycles, world traveling—his life was about fun and excitement, not the drudgery of having to live like a "normal person." And as I left Alabama and headed for Detroit so that I could train and try out for the Lions, I was convinced that that was the kind of life I, too, would have. It just *had* to be that way.

As a free agent, I'd been a little worried that I'd have a hard time getting a team to sign me, because I'd played sporadically at Alabama and my "barroom brawler" reputation was known far and wide. Coach Bryant had once told a pro scout that I was the guy you'd want with you if you got into a fight in an alley. Now, in some ways, a comment like that is a recommendation, but on the other hand, the last thing any coach needs is a loose cannon who is going to come in and disrupt the cohesiveness of the entire organization. Anyway, a guy I had played with at Alabama had become a sports agent who repped a few other guys I knew, and he made a few well-placed phone calls for me, vouching for my strength, work ethic, and determination. There hadn't been much negotiating, because no one on either side expected there to be much pay. Hell, I probably would have paid *them* to play—if I'd had any money, which I didn't, of course. Anyway, before I knew it, I was on my way to the Lions' training camp.

Detroit in 1981 was no longer the economic powerhouse it had once been, nor was it yet the scary ghost town we see on the news today. It didn't really matter much to me anyway, to be honest. I was so single-minded and focused on my dream that it could have been a war zone and I wouldn't have noticed, as long as I didn't actually get shot or something. Sure, it was a little intimidating that I was headed for a place where I knew no one. No ex-Alabama guys were on the Lions team at that time. I was just going to be thrown in with a bunch of strange players who were as good or better than I. But I had survived that experience when I transitioned from high school to college, so I had no doubt I could do it again. Though I missed both Tuscaloosa and all my friends there, I felt no sadness or depression. It was time to move on. You know, I can't remember if I went back to Savannah that summer or not. I can't even remember if I left a steady girlfriend behind or not. It was all about my next big conquest, not the past.

I found the practices in Detroit, compared to the practices at Alabama, pretty easy. But then, was there *any* pro team whose practices would have been as brutal as those I suffered through in my college days? I highly doubt it. You see, when you hit the pros, they start to teach you that football is—or should be—as much about the brain as the brawn. Professional playbooks are so complicated, so intricate, that there is necessarily a lot more class time than you have in college. These "skull sessions," as we called them, took up a big chunk of our day. Offensive meetings, defensive meetings, special teams meetings... Combine all that stuff with practice and you've got more than a full-time job. It's your whole life (well... *almost* your whole life, as you shall see).

The head coach of the Lions at that time was Monte Clark. After playing offensive tackle for both the Dallas Cowboys and the Cleveland Browns,

Clark had worked as an offensive line coach under Don Shula in Miami. The two of them transformed that team into an absolute ball of fire in the mid-Seventies, and then after a short stint with the 49ers, Clark was hired as the head coach of the Lions. He was a really nice guy, and we got along quite well. I always felt he appreciated my hard work and aggressiveness. His offensive coach, Fred Hoaglin, gave me lots of encouragement, too. So I was really happy with the coaching situation, and remained sure that I could convince them of my worthiness and earn a spot on the team. My height (6'2") was a negative in the position I was playing (offensive guard), and I would have to adjust to pro-type pass blocking, but those were not insurmountable problems.

As at Alabama, there was really no nutritional counseling for Lions' players. The feeling seemed to be that you were burning up so many calories that it just didn't matter where those calories came from, so there was no excuse for exceeding the weight requirements (for which you'd be fined $10 per pound). I had long ago done my own homework on the subject, however, and tried to eat a diet heavy in proteins and low in carbs. But while the food situation was pretty much the same at both places, the water situation couldn't have been more different. At Alabama, we got liquid maybe once every practice, and it was often some kind of nasty Gator-Aide mix in pathetic little Dixie cups. Don't ask me why; you'd think that even back then, they would have known how dumb and downright dangerous that was. But in Detroit, you could have water, fresh cool water, as much as you wanted. Between that and the lack of oppressive Southern heat, practices were far more comfortable then I had even thought possible.

The facilities in Detroit were better than at Alabama, but that's not really saying much. Oh, they weren't bad—don't get me wrong. But they were just typical pro facilities, nothing to write home about. There was nothing elaborate or plush about the locker room or the weight room, and the same could be said of the dorms at a nearby community college where we were housed. There was a curfew enforced at the dorms, but guys were always sneaking out and back in again, and the fine for doing that ($500) was a lot higher than the fine for gaining an extra pound. Fines, fines, fines. Everything was fines. You took your chances and sometimes you got away with it, but sometimes you didn't.

So my life appeared, on the surface, to be filled with possibilities. But what my coaches and my parents and the vast majority of my friends didn't know was this: I was taking steroids and my cocaine use was escalating, and there is no doubt in my mind that these drugs were magnifying some of my worst characteristics. Though I had always seemed to have an excess amount of testosterone and was no stranger to the occasional physical confrontation, up until that time, most people who knew me thought of me as a fun, outgoing guy—not someone who was frightening or dangerous. But now, not only did I feel a change inside me, I also felt a different vibe coming off of the people who'd react to me when I'd walk into a public place and immediately start throwing my weight around. I wanted everyone in any place I was to acknowledge my superiority. I wanted to control every situation, and I didn't want anyone to think they had anything to say about it. If a fight didn't come to me, I'd start one, just so I could feel like a big shot and have a story to blab all over the locker room the next day.

I sure got myself a story one night when an African-American buddy— a former player at Mississippi State—and I were leaving a Detroit nightclub in the early morning hours. The parking lot was dark, very dark. I got into my car on the driver's side and he got in on the passenger's side. It was a hot summer night, so we rolled our windows down, and that's when the car was approached by two drunken white dudes who were obviously looking for trouble. I had a heavy beard and probably the deepest tan I've ever sported, and when the racial epithets started to fly in the plural form, I realized that these guys thought *both* my friend and I were black.

"Hey, niggers!"

Oh, boy. I never did have the least amount of patience for racist jerks who said things like that, so you can imagine how much leniency I gave them when I was all cranked up on steroids, coke, and booze. Answer: none. When they started reaching though the open windows and grabbing at the locks, my friend and I knew we were about to be beaten or robbed or both, and we weren't having any of it. We swung into action and when it was all over, those punks were laid out on the pavement, unconscious. Blood was everywhere, pools of blood. I had bashed a head against hard metal. I had slammed an arm in a door. I had administered a beating like none I'd ever given before. We got out of there fast, because we knew those guys were hurt bad.

How bad? We didn't know the extent until the next day, when Coach Clark announced that two men were in a nearby hospital as the result of the actions of two Lions' players. If he knew that much, he probably knew it all, but he wanted us to own up to it voluntarily: "Will the two guys who were responsible for this please step forward?" We did. My drinking buddy and I were immediately released from the team with the explanation that the Lions simply could not deal with such negative publicity. I didn't protest. I'd been caught, and I'd take my lumps.

Though Coach Clark was not at all happy about the club incident, he must have seen enough good in me to want to give me a second chance, because he sent me down to a place where he had great connections: Miami. But after a week of training with the Dolphins, I was released in the next-to-the-last cut. And then, believe it or not, the Lions re-signed me as a free agent. I did pretty well this time, but I still got cut again. The sting of it was taken out, however, with an almost immediate offer that I found very intriguing: I was asked if I'd be interested in playing for a new spring league, the United States Football League, which would be getting started in January of 1983. Birmingham was going to have a team in this league called the Stallions; did I want to be a part of this team? I sure did. I was very grateful to the coaching staff in Detroit for helping me get into the USFL, and I was happy with the training I'd received. I accepted this offer right away.

In the months before I left for Birmingham, I went back to Savannah, where I worked during the day in a construction crew and bartended at night at an oyster bar called W.G. Shuckers. It was also during this time that I officially became the strongest man in Georgia. The morning of the bench press contest, I got up hung over because... well, because I got up hung over every morning. But it was nothing a six pack of Bud and few lines of cocaine couldn't fix. I walked into that contest a substance-soaked behemoth and pressed 560 pounds, breaking the state record. *"See?"* I told myself. *"You must be doing something right."* It was just a combination of youthful craziness and dangerous denial, of course. In truth, I was developing a mentality that would later crush me. I had put all my eggs in one bag, and I was poking holes in that bag with cocktail skewers and coke razors. The holes may have been tiny, but they were adding up, and the ultimate rupture was inevitable.

CHAPTER EIGHT

I LEFT FOR DAYTONA BEACH in February of 1983 to train with the Birmingham Stallions. They put us up in some pretty nice condominiums, like four guys to a condo, so that was nice. But the sports facilities were a little primitive, and we had about 100 guys trying to work out of a baseball locker room. I mean, we were *crammed* in there, with two or three players sharing a locker. Just getting your ankle taped was a big production, because you first had to find a place to actually sit down! So the coaches started weeding out the weaker people pretty quickly and pretty ruthlessly, trying to get those numbers down. They ran us ragged in hard, hard practices, and out of the initial hundred, only about 45 players were left when we headed for Birmingham.

The head coach of the Stallions was Rollie Dotsch. Dotsch had worked for the Pittsburgh Steelers and really knew his stuff. Despite his constant yelling and screaming (which he somehow always did with a cigar in his mouth), he was known as a "players' coach," and I just loved him. He drove us hard and was extremely demanding, but having played under Coach Bryant, I was used to that type of personality and it didn't bother me a bit. I worked my butt off at those practices in Daytona Beach, and everything was going just fine until I slipped one day and fractured my elbow. I was put on the injured reserve list just as we left for Birmingham.

I tried not to get too down about the injury. I was thrilled to be back in Alabama, where I'd become one of the heroes on a legendary team and where I still had so many friends and admirers. The injury would heal and I would play, I told myself, but in the meantime, there would be plenty of time for partying, nightclubs, women, and drugs, drugs, drugs. I was using huge amounts of steroids and legally-prescribed pain medication, but my thirst for pharmaceuticals was not yet quenched. Soon I made arrangements to have access to a pharmacy outside Birmingham—total access. It was an almost weekly routine for me to visit this place and "go shopping," buying jugs and bottles of whatever I wanted. And then of course there was the cocaine, which I was also doing daily.

Even after my injury healed, I was going hog wild on all this stuff. I thought nothing of staying out all night drinking at the Birmingham clubs, getting absolutely no sleep, and then swallowing and snorting God knows what in tremendous amounts to get through our next practice. It was sheer madness. I don't care how young you are, I don't care how strong you are… A human being just can't live that way without turning himself into a monster. It might be sooner, it might be later, but it will happen. At the time, however, I didn't see anything resembling a monster. I saw a guy who was on a new team that was pulling in big crowds at Legion Field in Birmingham. The stadium held 80,000 or so, and we would regularly draw 30 or 40,000. It all looked like success to me.

The great Jesse Owens once said, "Friendships born on the field of athletic strife are the real gold of competition. Awards become corroded, friends gather no dust." I made lots of friends while I played for the Stallions, and we had some great times together, traveling the country for road games and enjoying a bright spotlight in Birmingham. I lived with two other players who loved to party as much as I did, and in our Cadillacs we would cruise from one hot nightspot to the next, never worrying about the clock or overindulgence. Many a time I walked out of an after-hours bar at ten or eleven in the morning, the hard liquor still coursing through my system and the live music still ringing in my ears. My friends and I were rollin' hard and I was loving it.

My performance that year for the Stallions was pretty good, but not great. Every time I'd injure myself, the partying would escalate and the inevitable would happen. So when the USFL held an expansion draft for the '85 season, the Stallions didn't do a whole lot to hold onto me. It hurt, but the fact that I was the first offensive lineman taken by the Houston Gamblers gave my ego the little bump it needed. I didn't want to leave Birmingham. I had so many friends there, and I loved my adopted state. I wasn't too crazy about having to reinvent myself once again, but at least I would be playing ball and if I was lucky, perhaps I'd find a way back into the NFL. Soon I was on my way to Houston and my new home, a Hilton hotel. My steady girlfriend at the time was what we then called a "steward-ess," so I figured she could just as easily fly into Houston as she did into Birmingham, and she did.

I've burned out a lot of brain cells since Houston, and to be honest, I don't remember all that much about the city itself except that it was hot, the traffic sucked, and it was the biggest city I'd lived in up 'til then. How I felt about the city didn't really matter all that much; it was enough to know that quarterback Jim Kelly was going to be our big franchise player, that Jack Pardee (one of Bear Bryant's famed Junction Boys) was the head coach, and that Bob Young of the St. Louis Cardinals would be in charge of offense. I was especially excited to be a student under the direction of Coach Young. So, despite the sadness I had about leaving Birmingham, by the time I got to Huntsville for the Gamblers' training camp, I was psyched and ready to go.

The owner of the Gamblers was a dentist-turned-football-agent named Jerry Argovitz. To say that Argovitz was "flamboyant" would be a vast un-derstatement. The man loved attention, and didn't bother worrying whether that attention was positive or negative. Like Al Davis of the Oakland Raid-ers, he felt that all publicity was good publicity, and maybe that wasn't the best message to impart to an already out-of-control hellion such as myself. If Argovitz wanted publicity, I could give him plenty of it, and as soon as we started training I started making new party friends and carousing as often as I was able. Only problem was, training was in Huntsville, not Houston. This wasn't a big, glamorous party town. This was a small Texas town that revolved around a prison and a town whose citizens and law enforcement agents had a definite "hang 'em high" attitude. So when I went out to paint the town red on the first night of no curfew, the stars were aligned for some serious stuff to go down.

Coach Pardee had warned us at the after-dinner team meeting: "If any-body gets in trouble tonight, these nights without curfew will be ending." That was my cue to start snorting cocaine and drinking heavily, and I began working my way through the bars of Huntsville, which were often filled with underage kids from Sam Houston State University. When my friends and I wound up at a bar full of pool tables, I turned to one of them and said, "I bet you a thousand dollars I can go over there and get under that pool table and squat it." Why not? I weighed about 330 pounds, had a mere 7% body fat, and was officially the strongest man in all of Georgia. Oh, yeah, I could squat that table! But first I had to clear out the guys who were playing on it, and when I announced my intentions and began raking the balls into the pockets, they fought back. Eventually the bouncer and the owner came over, and after I told them I could whip them, a teammate hustled me out of there pretty quickly. The police had been alerted and were right outside the door, so as we passed them I feigned innocence and said, "You'd better hurry up and get in there; there's some guy causing all kinds of problems."

We got to my car and hit the road as fast as we could, but our escape was not to be. The police were onto us and followed us to the next bar. Noting their presence as we walked toward the door, I said, "Guys, you'd better get inside. You don't need this." The words were barely out of my mouth when one of the cops yelled "Freeze! Don't move!" He then ran up to me and I decked him in the mouth and knocked him out. His partner came from the other side and I turned and did the same to him. As they both lay on the ground unconscious, two more police cars pulled up and this time they had a dog with them. My teammates were in the club and I was on my own, so I took off running down the dark street. Oh, the screaming and the bark-ing! The dog caught me by the pant leg and I couldn't shake him off. The cops started beating me with their nightsticks, but I felt no pain and just kept cussing them out. Finally they got me on the ground, slammed my head on the asphalt, and cuffed me. My immobility didn't stop my mock-ing laughter, however, which just made it worse, and they continued to whale on me with those nightsticks. The more arrogant and obnoxious I became, the more pissed off and violent they became, but finally they threw me into a police car and hauled me off to jail.

I was booked for assaulting two officers and tossed into a holding cell that was overcrowded because it was a weekend. And I was delighted to see that some of my new friends were burly, cranky bikers who were looking for a target. One came over to me and started mouthing off, and I knew worse was coming if I didn't get out there. My solution? Faking insanity. I raved like a lunatic and paced the cell like a caged panther until the bikers screamed to the guards, "Get him out of here! He's nuts! He's insane!" In the resulting private cell, alone with my thoughts, my mind wandered back to my past as it had so many times before. I thought of the day when, as a child, I went to a neighborhood gathering place and saw a makeshift trough, like a pig's trough. Painted on its side as big as could be were the words "BILLY'S TROUGH." Before I could even absorb it visually, I heard the taunting from people who I had thought were my friends: "That's where Billy eats! He's a fat pig!"

There's no excuse for my adult violence—none— but there *were* childhood motivations, and those motivations were simply not being dealt with. Instead, they were being subsumed in a sea of drugs and alcohol. I couldn't forget those who had bullied me, and I was going to lash out and give them a hellish payback—even if "they" were the wrong people, people who weren't even there and had no idea why this enormous ball of rage was coming at them for no apparent reason. I finally fell asleep—or passed out—that night in my private cell, and when I awoke, a detective was railing at me through the little slot in the door. "Do you make a habit of going around beating up policemen?" he asked me. I replied, "I've already gotten two of you. Why don't you come on in here and find out?" By this time, the media was all over my arrest, and friends and acquaintances all across the country soon began hearing weird rumors, like the one about me "beating up a police dog" (which was not true and which I deny to this day).

My bond had been set pretty high. I called offensive coach Bob Young to come bail me out. He and everyone else on the coaching staff were *beyond* pissed off. They sure didn't want to hear about how Jerry Argovitz loved all publicity, good or bad. But amazingly, I was not immediately let go. Instead, I went back to practicing with the team, with one interesting difference: From that point on, there were always one or two police cars hanging around training camp. Sometimes the cops would circle the training area slowly and menacingly; other times they'd just park and stare intently through their dark sunglasses. But neither I nor anyone else there had any doubt who they were keeping an eye on: me. This passive-aggressive harassment went on and on, and while I don't feel sorry for myself, I am sorry that it affected the coaching staff and the other players. It's disturbing and creepy to be watched constantly.

Needless to say, the "bar thing" put me in a really bad place with head coach Jack Pardee. I don't know why he just didn't get rid of me right then and there, but he didn't. Instead, he allowed me to start the season, but then I suffered several bad injuries—first my calf, then my groin. When you take a lot of steroids, your muscles become so strong so quickly that the rest of your body has no time to catch up to them. Your joints, you tendons, and your ligaments become very stressed out from your muscles overworking them, and the injuries start piling up. That's what was happening to me. Finally, after a disastrous game in Chicago, where I played dragging one leg behind the other, Pardee called me into his office and told me that he was disappointed with my performance and that I wasn't giving 100%. I tried to argue, but he "gave me the hand" and said that he was going to demote me to the practice squad. "Cut me or trade me," I replied. "I don't care, but I'm not going to work on the practice squad." Wow, was that a stupid thing to say, or what? But I'm sure you're not surprised at this point.

So, five or six games into the Gamblers' first season, I was out of there. Didn't know where I was going to go or what I was going to do. And the worst part of it was, I couldn't just leave Texas and stay gone. I had all that legal drama in Huntsville ahead of me. When I went home to my parents' place in Savannah, a bail bondsman would call and harass us, accusing me of "jumping bail" because I was living in Georgia. Dad would grab the phone and yell, "You just send a bounty hunter here and you'll realize what Savannah's all about!" Oh, that Dad. What would I have done without him? He told me to set an appointment with the "lady judge" and throw myself at her mercy, which I did. Later, he went back to Huntsville with me (and my mom and my girlfriend) to talk privately with the DA. Going in, I didn't know if I'd be leaving there with my family or heading off to prison, as the DA wanted me to plea bargain for a year in prison.

But eventually Dad wore the DA down. I gave the two assaulted cops a cash settlement of 10,000 bucks each, and the judge warned me to get out of there and never come back to her state again. That was just fine by me. In all the years since, I've never had a problem steering clear of Texas.

CHAPTER NINE

AFTER MY LONE STAR STATE ADVENTURE, I could have easily wound up living at my parents' house in Savannah, as I had before in my young adulthood. My relationship with them was okay, or at least it was with my mom. She was so gentle and easy-going that it was almost impossible to be rejected by her. As for Dad, well, as usual he wasn't around all that much on a day-to-day basis. He would have gone off to his partying and I would have gone off to mine.

And what a non-stop party Savannah was. My hometown might not have been all that fun when I was a fat kid getting picked on, but it was like a playground for young adults, and during earlier "down times" I had worked right where all the action was, on River Street. At night I had bartended at a place called W.G. Shuckers, a seafood restaurant. No one there had thought anything of me drinking right along with the customers, and to be honest, they hadn't thought anything of me vacuuming up massive amounts of coke, either. In the Eighties, it seemed like everyone was. One of the female bartenders at Shuckers introduced me to her boyfriend, who was a contractor who needed a carpenter's helper, so I'd been busy night and day. But I just did not want to go back to Savannah again. I wanted to look forward, not back. Luckily, a call soon came that would settle the matter.

My friend Bill Elko, who came out of LSU and had been drafted by the San Diego Chargers, called me up in early 1985 and said, "Hey, you need to come out to San Diego and try out for the team."

"Man, you've gotta be crazy," I replied. "I've been out of football for a while, and I haven't been working out, and I've been partying my ass off, and—"

"No, no, they're looking for offensive linemen and I've been talking you up. You've gotta call them."

I pondered the possibilities. No, I wasn't in the proper shape, but I knew I could be if given just a little time. "Okay, but I need about a month to get ready."

"Yeah, sure, but call them."

I don't remember exactly whom I spoke to first—scouting director Ron Nay or offensive coach Dave Levy—but I did call the Chargers. They said, "Look, we want to fly you out for a work out."

I knew that if I wasn't honest it would just mean trouble later. "I'm not ready to work out with you guys," I said. "It would be of no benefit to me or to you."

"Well, how long do you need?"

"30 days."

"Okay, that's cool."

We set up a date, I started working out, and a month later I flew to San Diego. I realized I'd have to take a drug test as soon as I got there, but that didn't stop me from snorting up half of Colombia on the plane. Don't ask me how I passed that test. I don't know and sometimes it's just better not to even speculate.

Elko was kind enough to open his home to me, and after I went out on the field and did some drills for the Chargers, they said, "We'd like to sign you to a free-agent contract," and signed me then and there. Things seemed to be coming easily up until this point, but I wouldn't allow myself to just cruise along. I knew that the only possibility for me to make the team was to get noticed in a big way. Now, this may sound crazy to those working in today's football world, but I decided that I would stay on everyone's radar by starting a fight every day. The first opportunity I got, I hit a guy in practice. Blindsided him right out of the blue, as hard as I could. Everybody just kind of erupted. The coaches went crazy. People were screaming. It was quite the scene and, far from being humbled, I was already planning more of them.

However horrible my plan sounds now, it worked, but it came at a price I wasn't expecting. When my friend Bill Elko had called me out to San Diego, he was a defensive player, but during training camp, the Chargers not only switched him over to offense, but to the same offensive position that I was playing. Elko and I had been inseparable for months—living together, flying out to Vegas together, just hanging out together. Everyone had called us the "Brothers Bill" because we were so alike in our tastes and attitudes. But now we would have to compete for the same spot. Elko was, quite frankly, a better player than I, but he'd never played offense before so he was at a disadvantage. Then he hurt his foot and wound up getting cut. Talk about awkward. I felt like crap about it, but I now knew that I would make the team, and I had a job to do.

Leading us in our jobs was head coach Don Coryell, the first coach ever to win over one hundred games at both the collegiate and the professional level. He is now a member of both the San Diego Chargers' Hall of Fame and the College Football Hall of Fame, and I felt honored to play under him. I really loved Coach Coryell, and I know he liked my old-school playing style, even if my steroid-fueled violence sometimes spilled over into inappropriate situations. But the guy I had the most contact with, of course, was offensive coach Dave Levy. Levy was different from most coaches. The best word I can think of to describe him as is "cool," and it fits not only his temperament, but the fact that he coached in perhaps the coldest NFL game ever—the infamous 1982 "Freezer Bowl" in Cincinnati, where the temperature was minus nine degrees with a wind chill of minus 59. Levy treated players like grown adults, not like kids he was babysitting, and that usually resulted in them maturing under his authority. *Usually.*

When Levy's leadership was combined with that of veteran players like Don Macek, our center, and Ed White, a guard who was in his 18th year in the NFL, by the time I got to San Diego, it made for a powerful backbone to uphold the entire team. I was kind of shocked when Ed brought his 16-year-old son into the locker room and introduced him to everyone. Wow, some of the people I was working with were honest-to-goodness grown-ups now. Ed also had it together when it came to his career path; though he enjoyed a long, successful run in football, he knew there was more to life, and is now a painter and sculptor who is as passionate about his art as he was about his sport. In his days with the Chargers, Ed was kind of our offensive guru, and quite a character. His locker was next to mine, and it was fun to get to know someone whose personality was a little different than that of the average football player's. Ed was an excellent teacher.

Living and working in San Diego was great. I used to joke around with two other guys who came out of Alabama, Woodrow Lowe and Jesse Bendross, about what a breeze it was to practice and play in that town. And I do mean that literally; the wonderful dry air and moderate temperatures were heaven for players who had suffered heat and humidity for years on end. Woodrow, Jesse, and I stuck together as Alabama men and told our new teammates that Coach Bryant could stop the rain. A strip club was right down the road from the stadium, and I think I wore grooves in that road with my Harley Davidson motorcycle, my Mercedes 450 Sport 2-door, and my Ford Bronco. Oh, I could have saved my money like a smart person, but even though I knew my time with the Chargers would be short, I just couldn't stop myself from blowing it. It was a big decade with big money and big hair, and I was living large. It was also the waning days of the Cold War, and as I tooled around in/on my luxury vehicles I would often wear tee shirts with messages like "Kill a Commie for Mommie" or "Kill 'Em All and Let God Sort 'Em Out."

Did I believe in God at that time? I think I always did, deep down. I was frightened about the afterlife, but that fear never prompted me to actually do anything about changing my life here on Earth. My belief certainly didn't affect my abuse of substances or my sexual escapades with women, yet the latter was changing anyway in San Diego. It was over with the stewardess, and I was discovering a new and strange philosophy called "monogamy" with a California girl. She was a real sweetheart and very pretty, accompanying me down to Rosarito Beach in Tijuana about once a week to bask in the sun while drinking margaritas. Plus monogamy only covered "real sex," anyway. There was still that strip club down the road and plenty of flirting in bars and at parties. I could handle that.

One day after playing a preseason game, I was driving down the interstate listening to a sports report on the radio. They were listing all the players who had been cut that day from the Chargers, and right after that, they went into a story about the infamous bar fight that was still following me around. Unfortunately, the reporter could have used a few more journalism classes on the art of the segue—or maybe he'd attended too many. The transition was *so* fast and smooth that it was like, "Those cut are John Doe, Tom Snow, Joe Blow. [SHORTEST PAUSE IN THE HISTORY OF BROADCASTING] Bill Searcey…" I panicked and almost drove right off the road before I realized that I was *not* part of the first story, but just part of yet another "bad boy" story.

So, I was in for the season, and that season with the Chargers in San Diego was a big spit in the face to everyone who had ever said I couldn't do it. I was an NFL player. I was living the dream. I had tons of money and cool cars. And I was so strong that I was invited to stuff like the NFL Arm Wrestling Competition in Las Vegas. I didn't win it, but neither I nor anyone in America cared that I didn't win it. Despite what I did or didn't do on the field or in Vegas, my big and tough persona made me a popular guy who never lacked the kind of social connections that are so important in the world of sports. Sure, I didn't know what I was going to do after my pro career, but these people *loved* me. I was Bill, the gentle giant who could kill you with one blow if he wanted to, but who would rather hoist a beer and tell a few jokes. I'd always be okay, somehow, some way.

I've been asked if I think there's such a thing as a player being too "muscle bound." It's true that I was never as flexible as I could have been, and I think it was a combination of the training back then just not being as sophisticated as it is now and my obsession with my own strength. I just wasn't willing to give as much time and energy to speed and flexibility, and I didn't get a lot of feedback in that direction from above. On top of this problem, the next year they drafted a young offensive guard really high in the draft, which meant that they had a huge investment in him. I had gone into training camp that second year with a good attitude and had worked very hard in the off-season, but the bottom line was that better players were coming in. I was cut in mini-camp and my professional career was over. Deep inside, I knew I had nowhere else to go, because my bad reputation had only continued to grow and grow.

I had gone into that first year with the Chargers almost on a whim, because I'd had absolutely nothing to lose. Going into the second year that never was, I had a lot to lose—and no way of holding onto it with my big, strong, tough, rough hands.

CHAPTER TEN

WASH, RINSE, REPEAT. I packed up what I owned and rolled on out of San Diego. I knew I was totally lost. I had no idea of what I wanted to do, or even of anything I was *capable* of doing, other than football. I was broke and my truck was repossessed shortly after my split from the Chargers. Man, I just wanted to get on with my life. But where would I go? Alabama? No. Just as I'd once felt the need to move on from Savannah, I now wanted to move on from Alabama. My friends had finished school, gotten "real" jobs, and settled down. Though I enjoyed the attention I got for my college successes, in Alabama it almost felt like too much at times. I was too young to become a character in a Bruce Springsteen song, drunkenly rambling on about my glory days while everyone in the bar rolled their eyes. I wanted to focus on the future, not the past.

I don't remember *how* I wound up on Hilton Head Island, off South Carolina, but I sure remember *why*: Hilton Head was fun. Like my childhood stomping ground Daufuskie Island, Hilton Head had been settled by the Gullah people after the Civil War, but with its beauty, location, and twelve miles of beachfront, it was only a matter of time before the modern world intruded. Luckily, the first resort developer on the island, Charles E. Fraser, was a passionate conservationist, and his eco-friendly ideas about business were encoded in the Land Management Ordinance and are enforced by the Natural Resources Division. As a result, Hilton Head has much more tree coverage than most resort islands in the U.S., because buildings are actually built *around* the mature trees. This lush greenery gives it an almost magical aura, unlike any other place I've ever been.

Another thing for me to like about Hilton Head was all the rich people there, since I knew I'd be bartending or bouncing again and relying on their tips. Folks on this foot-shaped island love their drinking, feasting, and carousing, and they can afford to tip their service people well. Soon I had built up a little cash reserve and rented a condo with a chef and a bartender. So, I wasn't starving. In fact, I was surrounded by luxury. But as I walked around the parking lot of the bar at which I worked, Jim's Paradise, in the wee morning hours, picking up the beer cans and other trash left behind by those who had it all together, my thoughts were consumed by my recent failures. What was going on? How could it get any worse? Little did I know that it was going to get a *whole* lot worse, and as you can probably guess, drugs played a big role in that. I looked around and saw these wealthy people with their fancy toys, in their exclusive gated communities, and I wanted what they had. Well, now, there was only way I was going to make the kind of money I needed to get it.

Soon I was regularly driving to Florida to pick up dope from a dealer down there and transport it back to Hilton Head, where I would deal it from my home or even the from the bar at which I worked. When I was pressed for time, the Florida dealer would meet me halfway in Georgia, which I thought was pretty nice of him. But honor among thieves is a dangerous thing to believe in, and both he and I would soon regret our association. In the meantime, my roommates and I took to throwing wild parties at our condo. It was easy to get a big crowd of fun-loving twenty-somethings (and potential drug customers) there whenever I wanted. I'd stand at the door of the bar bouncing all night, telling every rowdy guy and every cute girl where the hot after-party would be held, and they'd show up in droves a few hours later.

I think that the very things that made Hilton Head so special were also the things that gave me delusions of what I could get away with there. When you're on Hilton Head, the outside world does not even seem real to you. It's so private and secluded. There's no poverty. There's no homelessness.

Even racism seems a non-issue as the descendents of the Gullah don their bright clothing, make their beautiful music, and explain their still-thriving culture to the happy, preppy white people. All this gives you a feeling of being protected, almost cocooned, and the last thing you can possibly imagine is being tossed into a cold jail cell for having a little coke on you. I was sure that as long as I was reasonably careful, I'd be safe. Of course, there's no way to be "reasonably careful" when you're dealing large amounts of cocaine. I was fooling myself.

One of the wealthy people on Hilton Head was Woody Baldus, who had made his money in sales for Bucyrus-Erie and then as the CEO of Terex Corporation. He lived on the island with his wife Kathleen and their three daughters: Karen, Kimberly, and Kelly. Woody had a big, beautiful place with a guest house, and he was building a second home right on the beach. The work ethic that had taken him to the top in business was something he instilled in his children, and that's why, when I met Karen in the summer of 1986, she was bartending, not lazing around like some spoiled rich girl. I had walked into this bar with my date for the night and another couple, but as soon as I saw Karen, I pretty much forgot about my date, and pestered the other girl in our party to go up to the bar and get Karen's phone number for me. Yeah, it was kind of obnoxious of me, but I got the number and I don't regret it. A beautiful girl with honey-brown hair and a knock-out figure doesn't come along every day, even in a Shangri-la like Hilton Head.

Karen had a lot more going for her than good looks, though. As I got to know her, I realized that she was one of the smartest people I'd ever met. She was working towards an advanced degree at the University of South Carolina after having earned a bachelor's at the University of Wisconsin-Madison, and she had plenty of ambition. This was definitely the kind of woman I was looking for at that point. Party girls and sports groupies are fun when you're sowing your wild oats, but almost everyone wants to settle down eventually. Soon after we started dating, I made it plain to Karen that I didn't want to see anyone but her, and we became inseparable. She was kind of a shy, serious person, but she was happy to follow me wherever I went and watch me make the usual spectacle of myself. And for quite a long time, she didn't realize the extent of my substance abuse, because everyone around us was partying hard, too. She thought I was just a wild and crazy guy, Mr. Fun.

The first time I went to the Baldus' home, I had to borrow a car to make myself look presentable. After parking it, I walked up the driveway and saw this kid sitting in one their cars, tears streaming down her face as she pounded her fists on the leather seats. When Mrs. Kathleen Baldus opened the door, I said, "Uh, did you know there's a little girl sitting in your car, crying?"

She shrugged and replied, "Oh, that's just Kelly."

The youngest daughter, Kelly, had had a fight with the middle daughter, Kim, and was pitching a fit about it because no one would give her any attention. From their mother's blasé reaction, it seemed like that kind of over-the-top drama was par for the course around there. Hmm… Maybe I would fit in.

I'm sure Karen's dad, Woody, wasn't too impressed with my long hair, my earrings in both ears, my borrowed car, and my complete lack of any future prospects. Could I blame him? This guy was everything I was not: a real establishment man who had played by the rules and the reaped the rewards. Of course he wasn't excited about his daughter dating me. (Much later, Karen told me that his first thought upon seeing me was, "Oh, s**t!") But like a lot of parents, he knew that forbidden fruit was all the sweeter, and that if he made a big deal out of it, Karen would only want me more. So he just kind of kept his mouth shut and hoped for the best. He was polite to me, and his wife was an absolute gem. I'd never met a mom like Kathleen, so crazy and fun. She was a great hostess and was always happy to feed me and put me up in their lovely guest house. I soon felt very comfortable at the Baldus's, and was really thankful to feel like part of their family. When Karen met my parents, it got even better, because they loved her right off the bat and she and my mom became good friends almost overnight. Our relationship just felt so right.

It felt right in spite of the fact that we were two very different people. I loved sports and working out. The only sport Karen was into was tennis, and she didn't just hate working out, she couldn't even stand the feeling of sweating. If she started sweating, she'd stop whatever it was she was doing and immediately shower. You can imagine how enthusiastic she was when someone approached me to get involved with pro wrestling. "Listen, you could make a lot of money in this thing," he said, so I actually started working out with some wrestlers and made contact with several other executives in the business. I was goofing around in the wrestling room one day when I had a freak accident in which I destroyed my ankle and my big toe was pointed back towards my heel. They rushed me to the hospital where surgeons reconstructed my ankle. That ended the wrestling thing and Karen was very relieved.

I had gone down to Tampa Bay shortly after meeting Karen and worked out for the Buccaneers. I benched pressed 225 pounds about 37 times, but they still didn't sign me. Then the Atlanta Falcons called me during the NFL strike and wanted to know if was interested in playing for them, but the ankle injury made it impossible and that was the last contact I ever had with the NFL. In some ways, I was okay with it being over. It wasn't the actual playing of football that I missed. I missed the people, the locker room, the relationships, the coaches, the recognition, the feeling of being a little different than the Average Joe. Oh, and I also missed the money—a lot. But as far as the game itself? I was just done, mentally and physically.

As smart as Karen was, she didn't catch on to my lies and criminal lifestyle for quite a while. Hell, I had lied to her right off the bat, not revealing that I was seven years older than she was because I thought she'd reject me. She eventually found out the truth about my age only because I accidentally left my driver's license out on a table at her apartment. And of course I lied to her about my cocaine dealing, too, but eventually it got to the point where one dealer was breaking into my apartment and waking me up with a gun in my mouth over a bad check (I talked my way out of it) and another dealer was threatening to call Mr. Baldus and ask *him* for the money I owed. Meanwhile, the undercover cops I knew from my work at the bar, the ones who had been tolerating my "second job" even though they knew all about it, were losing patience and looking to make some drug arrests. The jig was up, and I needed to get off Hilton Head.

Luckily, Karen had transferred to the University of Alabama-Birmingham during all this mess, so I high-tailed it south and, at her very strong suggestion, entered rehab for the first time.

CHAPTER ELEVEN

I N BIRMINGHAM, Karen and I lived in an apartment for a while, then moved into a house her father had put a down payment on. I got clean for the first time in my adult life, and had every intention of staying clean. Though I owed the IRS about $50,000 in back taxes, I had found a good job in the real estate business and knew I could pay it off. Being inducted into the Greater Savannah Athletic Hall of Fame had put some nice closure on my sports career and I was totally ready for the next chapter. But before we could even really start enjoying our new life, tragedy struck in both our families. Woody Baldus got very sick and died in November of 1991, only five months after being diagnosed with cancer. This was a huge blow to Karen and her family, and I tried to support them in any way I could, but soon I'd be facing the death of my own beloved mother.

It was sudden and unexpected. She'd had flu-like symptoms for a few months, and I was a little worried when I saw her that Christmas. Then, in February of 1992, I was on a flight to Detroit and called her from the plane. I always called Mom whenever I took a flight, because she just thought it was so cool that people were able to do that. But this time, Mom didn't answer; her housekeeper did. She informed me that Mom had been rushed to the hospital the night before with a very high fever and that I needed to come home. I got to the Detroit airport and turned right around.

When I got to Savannah, the doctors set up a meeting with me to tell me that she had been diagnosed with Stage 4 leukemia and that there was nothing they could do. My mother was terminally ill, and she didn't have long. I heard them, yet I was still just stunned at how quickly the cancer ravaged her body and killed her. I was at the hospital pretty much 24/7, and after three days of consciousness, Mom slipped into a coma.

One day when I was in her room, holding her hand, the nurse said to me, "Talk to her."

"She can't hear me," I replied.

"Oh, you'd be surprised. Lean over and talk into her ear and watch this monitor right here." So I did, and every time I'd say something, Mom's heart monitor would zoom.

I had told the doctors that if it got to the point where Mom was being kept alive by machines, I didn't want that, and that I would give the order to end it. Well, it got to that point, and they woke me up in the waiting room to tell me. Dad wasn't there with me. He hadn't been there much at all. He was in deep denial and he basically just fled the scene. I wasn't happy with him, of course, but I couldn't focus on that anger at the moment. I had to be there for Mom's sake and take care of the stuff Dad wouldn't or couldn't do. So, I told the doctors I was going to go home and make a few calls, and when I returned to the hospital, I would give them an answer. But by the time I got back, Mom had died, just five days after I had first walked through those doors. I was sad that I hadn't been with her at the exact moment of her death, but relieved that I didn't have to "pull the plug."

Now it was time to make the funeral arrangements, and again, Dad was incapable of handling it by himself—or handling it at all. He just collapsed when Mom died. He was like a zombie, shuffling amongst us with a blank look on his face and a tumbler of booze in his hand. Thank God Karen was there for me, and having just gone through the loss of a parent herself, she knew just what I was feeling and how to comfort me. It was a horrible time, that year, but ultimately, it brought us closer together. And I felt good that I had faced my mom's death without running back to alcohol or drugs. Could it be that I was at long last growing up?

Only a month or two after Mom's death, Karen told me that she thought she was pregnant. Because of some medical issues she had, doctors had told her that pregnancy was highly improbable, if not totally impossible, so we hadn't been "careful," and this was a real shocker. After we confirmed it, Karen was pretty freaked out about it, but I was nothing but happy with the news right from the start. We had just faced all this death, and I felt ready to celebrate a new life. It was amazing to me that just months before, I had thought I'd wind up in prison or dead, and at times couldn't even work up enough self-esteem to care. Now I cared very much, and I did my best to calm Karen's fears about pregnancy and birth.

But I'll admit there was one thing I was a little afraid of: telling Kathleen Baldus that I had gotten her daughter pregnant out of wedlock. Kathy had been through the wringer over her husband's death, and we didn't want to upset her any more than she already was. But the pregnancy was advancing, and I figured since she had to be told, I'd stop trying to find the perfect time or the perfect way to say it and just blurt it out, like the verbal equivalent of ripping a Band-Aid off her skin. My time to blurt came when Karen and I were visiting her in Hilton Head. Kathy walked into the bedroom at the guest house one morning and woke us up, and before I was even fully conscious I looked at her and asked, "Kathy, how would you feel about being a grandmother?"

She was kind of bustling around the room, and it seemed to go right over her head. "Oh, I don't know. What do you guys want for breakfast?"

"No. Kathy. How would you feel about being a grandmother?"

"Wait... Why?"

"Because you're gonna be one."

She was just as freaked out as her daughter at first, but quickly came around and joined us in our joy and excitement. Karen's sisters were very happy about the news as well. And even though Karen's dad and my mom were no longer with us, we all felt that this was kind of a special blessing from them.

It was time to get married. I regret that there was no romantic proposal; we just both kind of felt that the pregnancy sped up the inevitable, so the decision was more sensible than sentimental. Karen came from a Catholic family, but the Catholic Church does not allow for the kind of outdoor wedding on Hilton Head that we wanted, so we hired a Methodist pastor to marry us. Things got off to a bad start when I arrived five minutes late for a meeting with him after rushing off to Beaufort to pick up the marriage license (and getting a speeding ticket for my troubles).

"Obviously, you're not very serious about this wedding," he said as I bounded into the room.

Karen got this look on her face, like, *"Okay, not the right thing to say,"* and I started reaming the guy a new one. Within second, this pastor and I were all up in each other's faces, Karen was crying, and the wedding date was in peril. But we all calmed down in the next few days, and our beautiful wedding went off without a hitch. The whole wedding party took a boat to Daufuskie Island for the rehearsal dinner, which was so casual that we guys were wearing shorts. For the wedding itself, we had a big tent with a chandelier set up by the pool at the Baldus' beach house. My cousins served as my groomsmen, and my best man was Rich Wingo, a teammate at Alabama. Everybody else drank and got a little wild, but I didn't mind abstaining. I felt perfectly happy about the day itself and the direction in which my life was heading.

Karen's pregnancy was rough because of the medical issues I mentioned. She had horrible morning sickness and had to visit the doctor once a week because of various risk factors. She was put on bed rest at four months along. The weight of the baby became excruciatingly painful for her. She was hooked up to a monitor every night, and the docs would call us into the E.R. at all hours if they saw anything threatening. They were attempting to medicate her without harming the baby. They knew the child would come early, but they were trying to get him as strong as they could before the birth. By the late stages of her pregnancy, Karen was totally exhausted, and with work, running back and forth from the hospital on a near-daily basis, and doing all the cooking and household chores, so was I. If it weren't for the amazing doctors and nurses at Brookwood Medical Center in Birmingham, I don't know what we would have done. They were the ultimate professionals, and I always felt we were in the best of hands.

I was pretty calm during the birth, but Karen... Well, she was the mother of this tiny little person, and it was going to take a while for her to believe that we all were out of the woods. Our son, Woodward Alexander Searcey (after Karen's father and the middle name of both me and my father), born two months early and weighing about three pounds, stayed in the ICU for ten days. But he was never sick, just tiny. He fit in the palm of my hand, which was an absolute mind-blower for me. Yes, this was the kind of mind-blower that had replaced the ones I used to get from alcohol and illegal drugs, and I couldn't have been more thrilled about it. After we brought Little Woody home, I took off work for a short period of time to help Karen get into a routine, then headed back to the grind.

With the new addition to our family, our home started feeling a little too small. Karen had always had a dream of having a home in the country, and since I was making pretty good money, it was time to make that dream come true. We bought some acreage in Chelsea, Alabama, which is about ten miles outside of Birmingham, and we worked hard to create a place exactly like what she had always wanted. The house was old, but we gutted it and installed all the modern amenities. There was a big lake in front of the house, and a nice barn for Karen's horses. Dogs and cats and geese and every other kind of animal you can imagine ran around the property, and it was all encircled by a white fence. By the time we finished that place, it looked like something out of a Hallmark Hall of Fame Christmas movie.

Some of our neighbors in the country were friends, but mostly we just hung out as a family. We were busy with our renovation work for years, and most weeks I traveled Monday through Friday for my work. When we met, Karen hadn't been much of a football fan, and it was funny that she'd transferred to a university in Alabama, because she wasn't even sure they had electricity there yet. But she grew to love the state and become a die-hard Alabama fan, and after meeting my old teammates and their wives at various functions, she encouraged me to keep up with them and not let our friendships slide. In fact, in all that time, I can only remember one friendship that Karen encouraged me to end. It was an old buddy of mine whom she thought was a "bad influence." But I didn't end the friendship. I knew very well that no outside force even came close to being as bad an influence on me as I was on myself, and that my sobriety rested on my shoulders alone.

CHAPTER TWELVE

MY FATHER, who had been so shattered by my mother's death, somehow managed to go on for seven years without her, but he was never the same. He seemed so lost and broken, and even the birth of his grandson didn't reignite the fiery passion that had once been his most marked characteristic. He never came to visit us in Birmingham; I'd have to pack baby Woody and his things into my car and drive to Savannah to see him. I didn't mind the traveling, but I did mind the estrangement, which only continued to get worse. When Dad died of complications from throat cancer on April 8, 1999, I was surprised to learn that he'd been living in Palm Harbor, Florida for two years. That's how bad it was. His sisters made all the funeral arrangements, and I didn't try to take control. He had died a bitter, unloving shell of his former self, and I preferred to remember the brilliant, flamboyant, bar-hopping, pontificating, larger-than-life man he had once been. The man who had loved me, even if imperfectly.

Luckily, I was feeling the love in other areas of my life. Karen and I were having a great time raising our son. I won't lie and tell you I hadn't been hoping for a boy. It wasn't just the sports thing, though that was a definite factor. I really felt that with my history of failed anger management, my having a daughter might not be a good situation. Red flags went up whenever I thought about the teen years and dating issues. Though I had never witnessed anything really horrible like violence or rape against women in my college or professional years, I still knew a certain kind of man all too well, and I just knew I'd be overprotective. It would have been a constant stressor for me and completely unfair to my daughter. Besides, Karen wanted a boy as well. She'd grown up with two younger sisters, so she'd already had plenty of "girl drama" in her life. She was ready to try something different.

Raising Woody was one area in which Karen and I really never had any disagreements. We baptized him in the Catholic Church, but later took him with us when we attended a little Baptist church, not really making a big deal out of things like theology or denominations. We both agreed that since he was an only child and looked to stay that way, it was important to get him into daycare at an early age for socialization purposes. We also wanted him involved in sports, but only if that's what *he* wanted, and only if he had the dedication it took to stick with it. Most of all, after all I'd been through, we wanted Woody to be grounded in a good education, and to know that a well-rounded human being had the best chance for a full, healthy life.

Yes, things were going great at home, but they were also pretty wonderful at work. My old Alabama teammate Rich Wingo, who had later gone on to play with the Green Bay Packers, brought me into the real estate business after getting a rather desperate call from me. "Look, I'm in Birmingham, and I'm strung out bad on cocaine," I told him. "I can't get off it, and I don't know what to do. Can you help me?" Not only did he get me into a 30-day detox program, he then introduced me to Alex Baker, the president of the company he worked for. Alex took a chance on me and got me started as a construction manager, making about $30,000 a year. I instantly loved the job because I learned something new every day. Rich and Alex nurtured me, held my hand, and allowed me to make mistakes. They would correct me without destroying my confidence and they gave me the freedom to use my natural abilities.

I quickly realized that the very same natural charm that I had used so many times in the pursuit of debauchery could be used for all kinds of positive stuff like business deals, helping others reach their goals, building my own self-esteem, and making a comfortable living. I worked my butt off in construction, and after about seven years I was able to move into retail development, where I earned about $100,000 a year plus bonuses. The development business was exciting, and it became a passion for me. Like my father, I loved negotiating and haggling and arguing and drawing up contracts. Whether I was wheeling and dealing with the "big dogs" or helping an inexperienced tenant get a fair deal, I put my heart and soul into it. And I truly felt like I had a vision; I could look at a piece of land and just see the possibilities. Yes, I had finally found my niche.

Of course, not everything was smooth sailing all the time. There are some strange, crazy people in real estate development (and I can say that, because I was one of them), and like everyone else at my company, I had a few horror stories. One time, Rich and I were having an outdoor discussion with the associate of a vice president of a bank that had lent us the money to build a shopping center, and for some reason, this guy had a weird fixation on a patch of ground that had been seeded with grass but hadn't grown yet. I patiently explained that it was only a matter of weeks or maybe even just days, but it only seemed to make Mr. Associate even more upset. He went absolutely ballistic and started calling me a liar, and before I knew it, I was pushing him up against a car and Rich and the V.P. were pulling me off him and "helping" me to my own car. By the time we got back to the office, Alex had heard about the altercation, but he just laughed and joked that I had dislocated the guy's shoulder (which I hadn't).

Even worse was the time I tried to put together a deal in Lansing, Michigan. Walmart/Sam's Club had found a piece of property that they were very interested in, and they had tried to negotiate a fair purchase price, but the owner was extremely unreasonable, a real flake. So, they brought me in to try to get the deal done. The owner was Lebanese, so I of course tried to score points by immediately mentioning that *I* was half-Lebanese, but he didn't seem all that impressed. It took me six long months, but finally I convinced this guy to sign a contract and we started doing our due diligence work. During this due diligence phase, I spent about a million dollars of our company's money and dreamed of what the closing would mean for me. It was going to be my biggest deal yet, my biggest check yet, and Karen and I would finally be completely free of debt. But two weeks prior to closing, it all fell apart, and I had to walk into Alex Baker's office and tell him we weren't going to close—after spending one million dollars of his money!

I traveled a lot for my work, but that didn't bother me. I enjoyed going to new places and meeting new people. The traveling didn't bother my wife, either, because her father had traveled a lot and it just seemed normal to her. Also, she knew that no matter how crazy I got in other areas of my life, there was one area that just wasn't very tempting for me: adultery. Isn't it strange how different people are seduced by different vices? How one can grab onto you and never let go, while the other is fairly easily avoided? Not to mention how we tend to point the finger at others and say, "Well at least I'm not *that* bad!" My father's former colleague, President Jimmy Carter, told *Playboy* magazine in 1976, "Christ said, 'I tell you that anyone who looks on a woman with lust has in his heart already committed adultery.'" Carter was widely mocked for this statement, but his point was that as soon as a man starts letting himself off the hook by assuring himself that *his* sins are not as bad as those of his neighbors, he's in a lot of trouble. Yes, I was sexually faithful to my wife. But in the coming years, I would wound her in other ways that were just as painful and just as destructive.

Karen and I had always been so different. I was so spontaneous and wild that I was almost feral at times. Karen was thoughtful, serious, and methodical. Opposites attract, and in the beginning these differences were sexy and alluring. But as time went on, they began to wear on both of us. For example, whenever we went on vacation to Hilton Head, Karen would plan the trip down to the last minute. She needed to know exactly when we'd get there and exactly when we'd leave, and of course I agreed to that before we headed out. But then, I was there, back on my beautiful island, and the beach and the ocean and the Spanish moss worked their magic on me once again. So I would beg her to extend our time there, and she would rightly point out that we had obligations and responsibilities back home in Alabama. Neither of us was the Good Guy or the Bad Guy in all this; it was just a clash of personalities and opinions that slowly invaded every area of our life together.

We looked for a spiritual answer. When we didn't find it in the Catholic Church, we tried a Baptist church. We went to services every Sunday and attended Bible study classes, too. But looking back, I can see how there was a connection that was just not being made. It never really "clicked" in my head or in my heart. I was parroting the pastor and his followers, telling them what they wanted to hear. It's not that I didn't *want* to believe it. I looked around me and these people seemed to have the answer. But if there's one thing you can't fake, it's a spiritual awakening. Those around you may be fooled, but you'll never fool yourself. It's either there or it isn't, and deep down I knew it wasn't. Eventually Karen and I just stopped going to services, though we never officially left the church.

Thank goodness there was one thing I didn't have to fake, at least for the first seven or eight years or so: being a good father. I loved our son with all my heart, and I loved spending time with him. It was no chore to fulfill my paternal "duties." It was a real joy, just hanging out with my kid and seeing the world anew through his tender eyes. (Heaven knows that was something *my* jaded eyes needed!) Coaching Woody and his friends in Little League football was a lot of fun, though like any former player who had once risen to uncommon heights, I had to remind myself now and then, "Uh, Bill, these kids aren't necessarily future All-Americans, okay?" I hope I emphasized commitment and work ethic without being too much of a psycho. There is nothing more annoying to other parents—and even potentially harmful to the self-esteem of children—than an overbearing Little League dad. I just tried to relax and put it in the proper perspective.

So while I was never Ward Cleaver, I felt I was doing a pretty good job of being a husband, father, and businessman. I got the affection I needed from an imperfect, but still-strong marriage. I got the maturity I needed from nurturing my growing son. I got the dignity I needed from doing a hard day's work.

And then I got sick.

All-American at Benedictine Military School in Savannah, mid-Seventies.

At the Georgia State Senate with Dad.

As a Georgia state senator, Dad (right) may have strongly disagreed with Lester Maddox on desegregation, but he wasn't going to let that stop him from partying at the governor's mansion! (That's Mom on the left)

And as Assistant District Attorney of Savannah, Dad entertained many jurors with his theatrical style as he put the bad guys away.

Playing for Alabama.

National Champions: Roll Tide!

With some teammates on the cover of TIDE *(lower left).*

*A candid I took of Coach Bryant in our luxurious locker room.
(This is the part where I slap my hand on my knee and say,
"Back in my day…!")*

Legion Field Birmingham
November 29, 1980
Price $1.00

We cleaned up real good, didn't we? (I'm in the back row, fourth from left)

Coach at the height of his fame.

Giving Coach a run for his money in the girl department.

Partying with Gamblers teammates in Houston. (I'm seated).

In San Diego, when I was with the Chargers.

With my best man, Rich Wingo (second from left),
and other Alabama teammates before my wedding ceremony.

Karen and I at our wedding…

…and later in our marriage.

With Baby Woody.

Four-year-old Woody with his first fish.

Before Heavy.

On the set of A&E's Heavy *(the Hilton Head Health Institute)
with some of the many friends I made there.*

After Heavy *(with my son, Woody).*

Back on my finger, where it's staying this time!

Today.

CHAPTER THIRTEEN

I T ALL STARTED SO INNOCENTLY, with a kidney stone. How insane is it that something so small could set me on a path of destruction that would cost me everything I held dear? But these tiny menaces are one of the most painful medical conditions a human being can have, and they've been torturing us for millennia. According to the National Kidney and Urologic Diseases Information Clearinghouse, "Scientists have found evidence of kidney stones in a 7,000-year-old Egyptian mummy." Back then, there was nothing to do about it but suffer, but when my wife rushed me to the hospital in early 1998, everyone involved expected that I'd be treated with pain pills, and no one thought a thing of it. Neither Karen nor I were worried about it. After all, as a young man I'd messed around with pharmaceuticals just like I'd messed around with pot, hash, acid, 'shrooms, and everything else under the sun, and I'd given them all up pretty easily. Cocaine was the only drug for which I'd needed rehab.

The thing is, despite my personal and professional success, I'd been depressed leading up to this kidney stone incident, probably more depressed than I'd even realized. Karen had urged me to see a shrink for some help, but I was the tough, proud jock who wouldn't hear of it. You know how hard it is to get the average guy to admit there's a mental or emotional problem; add a few decades of hardcore athletic training and sports idolatry and it's just not going to happen. My identity was that of a rugged individu-alist who had broken all the rules before finally deciding to play by their rules and *win*. Sure, I'd had help when it came to my muscles and bones, but when it came to my head and heart, I had gone it alone. I didn't need any coddling from psychiatrists or priests. That stuff was for girls and… well, dudes who weren't football players. Needless to say, this ridiculous attitude led to a repression of my feelings that ate away at me for years and led to the disaster I'm about to describe.

I was in a world of pain when we got to the hospital that day, and I'm not just talking about the kidney stone. Sure, when they hooked me up to that IV and the Dilaudid started dripping into my arm the torment in my gut began to disappear, but that wasn't what startled and amazed me. What startled and amazed me was the sudden evaporation of the heavy depres-sion that had been weighing down my entire body for what seemed like an eternity. People who have never experienced that kind of depression don't really understand how physical it is: how your neck throbs with constant tension; your limbs ache so badly you could cry; and your chest feels like it's being crushed by a boulder. It's an absolute misery that, when it's at its worst, can prevent you from even getting out of bed in the morning. But on that day in the ER, it sure wasn't preventing me from doing anything. Hell, I wanted to jump out of that bed and dance around the room. I wasn't even thinking about the kidney stone anymore. All I could think was, *"This is the answer to my depression. If I could duplicate this feeling all the time, everything would be wonderful."*

I didn't say that out loud, of course. Not to Karen, not to the doctors, not to anyone. In that very first moment, shame was already mixed into the relief, but the relief was so overwhelming that I just pushed the shame aside. I stayed in the hospital for several days to have surgery on the stone and was heavily medicated the entire time. When it was time to go home, they gave me prescription pills, which continued to keep the depression at bay. But when I ran out of those pills, it came roaring back with a vengeance. Panic and fear engulfed me. I had to get back to that feeling, no matter what it took. So I called the hospital and complained that the pain was still there, and got refills on my meds. I was off and running. Already I was thinking like an addict, plotting and planning how I would get more of this drug when I ran out in the mid-summer. I actually welcomed a back problem that came along soon after. The pain was real, so I didn't even have to lie when I went to a specialist for it. After administering pain blocks, he added Valium to the pills I was already taking for the kidney stone surgery like it was just no big deal. Although I was telling the truth about my back, this made me realize just how easy it would be to start faking illnesses and go "doctor shopping."

In the beginning, I was a highly-functioning addict, in part because my life had been set up in a way that I had very little responsibility on paper. Because of the credit and tax problems I'd brought to the relationship, everything Karen and I owned was in her name. I'd never gone to real estate school and was able to sell real estate under my company's license. The nature of my job called for lots of travel, and even when I was in town, I was always running in and out of the office. So when I started to play drug games during the workweek, it took a long time for my coworkers to notice that something was out of whack. And they weren't the only ones who didn't notice. It amazes me that I operated a motor vehicle in that condition every day for years and was never even pulled over once. I'd go to other cities, rent cars, and drive around high as a kite. I think the fact that I drank no alcohol at all at this time really helped me keep my substance abuse on the down-low. I didn't smell like I was doing anything bad.

After a few years, the list of prescription drugs I was taking was as long as my arm—Lortab, Xanax, Klonopin, Valium, and on and on. 20 to 30 Lortabs alone, every day, and whatever other pills I had on hand on top of it. I'd drink pharmaceutical cough syrup like water. All these drugs were legal, but the way I obtained them certainly was not. I made the rounds of all the emergency rooms in the Birmingham area. And almost unbelievably, many times—at least ten or eleven—there were stones that would show up in the scans to back up my claims. But it still got real dicey, because I was seeing the same doctors over and over, and they started recognizing me. Their suspicions growing, I was forced to widen my base and travel farther for my drugs. One time, in Philadelphia, Mississippi, I put too much blood in my urine and they made me take the test a second time—with a cop in the bathroom, watching me! My desperation reached ever higher levels; when I wasn't sneaking out of my home at 3:00 AM to visit a 24-hour Walgreens, I was buying liquid methadone on the black market.

But even my wife was in the dark about all this until my behavior got really bizarre. My mother-in-law Kathleen came to Birmingham for a visit, and because she suspected my drug problem she counted the pills in her handbag on the first day. Guess what she found—or didn't find—when she counted them again a few days later? She busted me, and it was quite an ugly scene. The eventual, on-and-off estrangement with Kathleen and other members of Karen's family was so terribly sad for all of us. They had become *my* family, the only family I had left. If I couldn't stop for myself, I wanted to stop for them. But I was too deathly afraid of the depression that I knew would return if I went off the drugs.

Our financial problems intensified, and I started pawning stuff from around the house. Tools. Karen's Rolex watch. Objects from the china cabinet. Once I pawned our wedding silver right before Thanksgiving (great timing, huh?), and when Karen went to make the holiday dinner...

"Where's our wedding silver?"

"What? I don't know."

"Bill, stop it. Did you pawn it?"

"No! Get off my back."

She picked up her cell phone. "So, if I call around, I'm not going to find our wedding silver in a pawn shop?"

When she started dialing the sheriff, I caved. "Yes, okay? It's at the pawn shop." Did I apologize? I don't even remember, and if I did, it wasn't worth much at that point. This poor woman had once had the University of Alabama recreate my National Championship rings for me after I pawned them to pay a drug debt, but that was early in our relationship, when she still believed in my redemption. Ever since she had played a message a pharmacy had left on our answering machine, telling me I could no longer obtain drugs from them, she had known what I was up to. Now she was at the end of her rope.

And she wasn't the only one at the end of her rope. I had become a liability to my company, and I knew it. Alex and Rich kept me on for much longer than they should have because they were my friends, but even the kindest friendship has its limits. I was nodding off at my desk. I was passing out in the fitness room, just passing out right on the damn floor. And then, in late 2003, I went to "look at a piece of land" in Mississippi. Translation:

I took off with a paycheck in my pocket and wound up at a casino in Mississippi. (Hey, I doubled my money!) I was AWOL for three days, and when I got back home, I was seriously messed up. I passed out after not sleeping for days, and when I woke up, I was in the backseat of a car. Karen and the pastor from out church were taking me to a psych ward in Tuscaloosa. After a few days in the psych ward, I took a month off of work, then returned—not in development, but back in construction.

In early 2004, I made a vow to kick up my enthusiasm and get things going in the right direction at work again. I was still under this delusion that I could handle anything. As much good as sports training can do for a young person, like anything else, it has its downside, and that was manifesting itself in my inability to reach out to others for help. How could I put my weakness on display like that? How could I cry for help like a little child? What would Coach Bryant and all my other coaches and fellow players think of me if they saw me admitting that a drug addiction was stronger than I was, that it was kicking my ass all over the place? Hadn't they taught me how to tough it out? (All these questions were just my sickness talking, of course. In reality, Coach Bryant had always told us that we were family for the rest of our lives, no matter what, and that we should take care of each other forever.)

Those former coaches and fellow players knew nothing about any of this, because I had pretty much given up all contact with them (aside from Rich). Sports, football, college and pro reunions… I didn't give a crap. Oh, I'd watch a game once in a while, my eyes glazed over and my mind muddled and my now-huge belly resting on my thighs. If anything, it just made me feel even worse to see those young men playing the game that had once been my life, so full of promise and taking such pure joy in it. And after the game, I'd do what I always did: avoid any mirrors in our bathrooms or bedrooms. I didn't want to see the obese, drug-craving body that had so betrayed me. I didn't want to see the blank, straight face that my family members and friends had to scrutinize when I lied to them. I didn't want to look into the eyes that no longer bore the slightest trace of the good humor I'd once been known for. My journey to self-loathing was complete, and if it hadn't been for my son… Well, I wouldn't have put a gun to my head and pulled the trigger. But a fatal overdose would have been just fine with me.

CHAPTER FOURTEEN

My WIFE AND I were no longer really speaking to each other, even though we still lived in the same house. She slept upstairs. I slept downstairs. At first we tried to hide our disagreements from our son, but as our anger grew, 12-year-old Woody saw and heard more things that he never should have had to witness. The days of family holidays and vacations were behind us. Karen would take off for Hilton Head with Woody in tow and leave me behind to my addiction, depression, and lethargy. I don't blame her, of course. If I'd gone with them, we just would have continued our fighting on the island, and her family surely didn't want to see me. They had begged and pleaded with me to stop my destructive ways for years, and they were exhausted and hurt.

Karen made it clear that she wanted a divorce, and I made it clear that I was just not going to allow it. No one was going to make me give up my marriage. No one was going to force me to walk away from my child. Now, obviously, there's nothing wrong with being anti-divorce, but the question is, where was my opposition to it coming from? Was it coming from a place of honor and healthy living, or was it coming from a place of dysfunction and control-freakiness? At that point, Karen was through being controlled. She would call me up at work and tell me that she was going to have me served with divorce papers there, and the vicious insults would begin again.

I shudder to think of the things we said to one another. In August of 2004, I finally agreed to sign the papers, but I told her, "If you want a divorce, you pay for it. I refuse to pay a penny for this because I don't want it. And you tell Woody, because I won't do that, either."

Soon after the divorce became final, I went on one of my last business trips and called home one night to check on Woody. "Hey Dad," he said, "Mom told me about the divorce."

"Well, what do you think?"

"I think it's good, because you won't scream at each other anymore."

But the screaming wasn't over yet. Yes, I was that person I thought I'd never be—a divorced man—but I was still living with my ex-wife and child because I had nowhere else to go. I knew the ax was going to fall soon at work, since I'd turned into a virtual hermit and could hardly ever even make it into the office. I slept, I took drugs, and I got fatter. That was my life. Sure enough, in October of 2004, my dear friend and former team-mate, Rich Wingo, called me into his office and fired me. He had tried so many times to talk to me about what he thought was my only hope—Jesus Christ—but I hadn't been ready to listen. The firing was heartbreaking for both of us, but I wasn't the least bit angry at Rich. I feel guilty to this day about forcing him to let me go after he'd tried so very hard to help me and keep me on at the company. And the sickest part of the whole thing is this: As bad as Rich and my other coworkers thought my addiction was, they *still* didn't know the half of it. They will be shocked when they read some of the stories in this book.

I didn't think it was possible for me to become even more depressed than I was, but it happened. The drugs that had once lifted my depression were now making it worse. Every time I'd think I had hit bottom, I'd find another bottom. Every time I'd think my actions couldn't be any more shameless and unethical, I'd lower myself yet again and attempt to comfort myself with more excuses. Those attempts failed miserably. I knew that I was committing serious crimes in my constant quest for drugs, and para-noia was running through me like a raging river. Everyone was against me. Everyone hated me. The whole universe was trying to screw me. Me, me, me. That total self-absorption is the one thing that all addicts have in common, and until it's broken, recovery is impossible. Outside forces can try to intervene, but to say they're fighting an uphill battle is a vast understatement.

Still, my caring ex-sister-in-law, Kim, tried to do what she could. In late October, she convinced me to detox once again. At first I thought, *What's the point? I've already lost my wife.* But I felt so sick and terrified that she was eventually able to get me into the rehab center. The effects of this shot at sobriety didn't last long, however. I was a basket case not only about the divorce, but also about the bankruptcy for which Karen and I had filed. There seemed to be no hope in any area of my life, and I couldn't face that in a sober state. Within weeks, I was once again lying and hiding and chasing my drugs, and I needed more drugs than ever. A monthly prescription for Lortab now only lasted me a few days. Though I wanted to live as a recluse, I had no choice but to throw my huge body all over the Birmingham area, pathetically prowling around like the common criminal I'd become.

Though I've forgotten many things because of the drug haze I was in, I'll never forget the day I found out that Karen was seeing another man. I realize now that she had every right to do so, but at the time, I absolutely flipped out. I stormed around the house, furiously tearing up our wedding albums and heaving a wedding portrait through a pane-glass window. My jealousy was out of control, and I screamed, yelled, and called her names that I won't repeat but that I'm sure you can imagine. Karen had been urging me to start seeing other women, and now I realized why. But a short time later, when she caught me talking to an old college girlfriend on the phone, it became clear that her feelings were confused. She went nuts on me.

"Will you stop it?" I said, holding my cell phone high and away from her. "I'm not even seeing this woman now. It was a million years ago, and she lives a million miles away."

I was actually telling the truth about it, but Karen didn't care. "If you won't give me *your* phone, I'll just call her on *mine* and tell her to pick you up!"

As I snatched her phone away from her, it hit me that she had jealousy issues, too, and though she wanted both of us to move on, she didn't want to *witness* me moving on. My fate was now sealed: Karen wanted me out, and she wanted me out immediately. She threatened to call the police and have me physically removed from our home. I raged at her, screaming that I had put tons of money and effort into the house, but I knew I didn't have a prayer, legally speaking. It was all in her name, and that was *my* fault, a result of my ill-spent youth. And while I had been lying around the house in my drug-induced stupor, Karen had been getting up every morning and going to work. Any last shred of sympathy for me was gone. She went upstairs and collected a pile of my clothes in her arms, then walked out the front door and threw them on the lawn. "Out! Get out or I'll call the police!"

This was it. It was finally, really happening. I collected some more of my clothing—and my drugs, of course—and shoved them into plastic garbage bags as my son cried hysterically and begged me not to leave. I was in such an awful state that I didn't know if I should try to comfort him or just get the hell out of there. He was an emotionally tortured kid who just needed this madness to stop. Even I knew that. I tossed my stuff into the backseat of my 1991 Mercury Marquis and then flopped down behind the wheel. As if I were in a scene from a bad movie, I peeled rubber out of there with tears streaming down my face and just drove around aimlessly for hours. Then in the middle of that rainy night, when I was sure Karen and Woody were asleep, I inched back onto our long, gravel driveway and slept fitfully in my car until sunrise. When I awoke, I knew I couldn't stay. But where would I go?

After sleeping in my car for a few days, the pastor at the church Karen and I had attended took me to a motel and told me that they would pay to put me up there for a month. If I'd been in my right mind, I would have been able to get my act together in that time. I had an opportunity to get disability benefits because of my depression, and would have gotten 60% of my salary. That would have been $60,000 a year for two or three years—I don't remember exactly how long. But I was in such bad shape mentally that I was not even able to fill out the forms. Though I knew I couldn't handle any kind of job, when my time ran out at the motel, I took one, for a neighbor of ours who built decks and porches. On the very first day, I fell backwards off a deck and tore the meniscus in my knee. I didn't care; the injury meant that I had to have surgery, which meant I could stay at the hospital and get plenty of pharmaceuticals with no questions asked. My kidney stone buddies came back strong, too. They never let me down.

On the operating table for my knee surgery, I died. I'm not being melodramatic; they put me under and were prepping me for the surgeon (an Auburn alumnus, ironically enough) when I just stopped breathing. They tried to get a tube down my throat, but something was blocking it and they had to resort to a tracheotomy. I woke up in intensive care, and as Karen was my emergency contact, hers was the first face I saw. She wasn't too enthusiastic about this duty, but what could she do? She was still the mother of my child. When the doctor told me that because of my near-death experience I had not even had the knee surgery, I didn't react as most people would, with disappointment. All it meant to me was that I'd have a roof over my head for a little longer. Didn't know how I'd pay for that shelter, but I'd figure that out later, like I figured everything out later.

When I finally had to leave the hospital, I really and truly became homeless, except for my "hooptie," the Marquis. Sometimes I'd go to the baseball park where Woody played Little League and break into the room above the concession stand where they held kids' birthday parties and stuff like that. There was a couch there that I could sleep on until the morning. Occasionally I would find a swimming pool to bathe in, then sleep on one of the lounge chairs that surrounded it. When I wasn't using one of those swimming pools for my hygiene, I was trying to clean my enormous body in gas station and convenience store restrooms or with garden hoses. The results were unsatisfactory, to say the least. Once in a great while, I'd get use a real bathroom, when I crashed at a friend's place. But those times were rare, because I had very few friends left.

Those few friends would at first lend me a few hundred dollars here or there for a motel room. Then a twenty here or there for "food" (translation: drugs). It was total chaos. I was scrambling to find shelter every day, and often times I just didn't find it. I needed to eat, of course, but every time I spent money on food, I thought only of the drugs I could have bought with it (or the booze; I'd decided I liked that again, too). With all this angst about food, you'd think I would have at least lost a little weight, but that didn't happen. I was still as big as a house and in complete dishevelment. I would wear the same clothes for God knows how long, because I couldn't afford to use a coin laundry. I'd run out of toothpaste and not have the two bucks it would take to replace it. I'd do a lot of things I'd never dreamed I'd do.

I was still making my pharmacy rounds, of course. I once walked into a little pharmacy in Mississippi to have a prescription filled and lo and behold, they had left a stack of prescription slips right out on the counter. Only one person was working, and when he turned his back, I shuffled through those slips and found one for about 100 Lortab. This was in addition to my own slip for Lortab. So I filled my prescription there, and when I got back to Alabama, I filled this other guy's prescription. In addition to the pharmacies, I was running my games at discount drug stores, returning items I'd stolen in order to buy drugs and food. Once when I needed gas, I handed the gas station owner my wedding ring and promised I'd be back to pay for it. I never went back. To this day I often wonder what he did with that ring that had once meant so much to me.

Many times during this nightmare, I thought of my parents and how they would feel about what had become of me. Mom had left me so quickly and tragically, and Dad had shut himself off from me when I had been in the most healthy phase of my life. I hate to sound like some pop psychologist, but there really hadn't been the "closure" that any of us needed. Now, the only person I had left—the only person who prevented me from just ending it all—was my son. After I became homeless, I called Woody on my cell every night before his bedtime to tell him I loved him. Over and over, both Karen and I told him that none of this mess was his fault. But thinking about the suffering I put him through during that time period haunts me. I fear I will never be able to make it up to him, and that our relationship might end the way my relationship with my Dad did.

So, here I was: a man who had several times, in several ways, reached the heights of worldly success, now a homeless addict, thief, and beggar. I was living up (down?) to all the prophecies of all those who had taunted me as a fat, ugly, stupid loser. The horrible things I'd done were returning to me tenfold. The chickens were coming home to roost, and I was the biggest chicken of all, too afraid to face up to the truth: My soul was gone.

CHAPTER FIFTEEN

THERE ARE OVER 600,000 homeless people in the United States. During my time on the streets in Birmingham, I only met a tiny fraction of that number, but it was enough to make an impression on me that will never fade. I saw heavily pregnant women dragging children behind them as they scrounged for food. I saw tiny infants who were practically born right on the street. I saw human beings living and sleeping under bridges, with no real protection from the harsh elements. I saw children who had never known any other home life than squatting in abandoned buildings. I saw the elderly and the disabled literally dragging themselves down sidewalks. Even a guy who was as wrapped up in himself as I'd become couldn't ignore that kind of misery in others.

One guy I knew during that time had a law degree and had been doing pretty well for himself until he became addicted to drugs. Petrified that he would harm someone by practicing law while high, he closed his law firm and surrendered himself to the streets. But unlike this guy and myself, some of the people I met hadn't really "done anything" to wind up where they were. The economy was tanking, the housing market was crashing, jobs were becoming scarce, and before they knew it, they were living out of cars and vans and desperately trying to claw their way back into a home.

Perhaps they made some lousy decisions or didn't always handle their money correctly, but they were not addicts or criminals. Yet their punishment was just as brutal as mine.

As bad as I felt for my fellow homeless ones, however, my priority remained the acquisition of drugs for myself. When I ran out of pharmacies and hospitals, I had no choice but to take my chances in the sordid, dangerous, underground drug world of Birmingham. There was one "organization" I was getting pills from almost every day, and the way they'd arranged their business, you'd almost think it was legit. They sure didn't do too much to keep it hidden; it was like a drive-up pharmacy for those who were getting pain medication without prescriptions. Their little shop was right on a main road, and when they opened every morning at daylight, there would often be a line of cars there already, with drivers and passengers hanging out the windows. I'd pull up behind them and a guy would walk out to my car and ask me what I wanted. They always had my main drug, Lortab, and Lortab was always seven bucks apiece. You could buy one Lortab or one thousand Lortab, it didn't matter: seven bucks apiece. This dealing was so flagrant that I find it very hard to believe the authorities didn't know what was going on, but they didn't seem all that interested and we weren't all that worried. It was bizarre.

If I'd had a choice I probably would have just curled up in the Marquis and waited to die, but I didn't have a choice. I had to be out on the streets in order to get my dope, so sometimes I'd run into people I'd known in my "real life." It was always so horribly awkward and embarrassing. Oh, I'd try to smile and chat as though nothing was wrong, but my situation was obvious to anyone with half a brain. These old friends and acquaintances would just look at me and shake their heads, wondering what on earth had happened, how I'd allowed myself to fall so far so fast. I could see they were shaken as they walked away, shocked by the dirty, nasty, fat guy who had once lived in their world, and had a real job, and had a nice family.

Some of my friends tried so hard not to abandon me completely. One of my old pals from the real estate business, Arthur, would let me come to his house every now and then, just to sleep in a real bed and take a real shower and launder my filthy clothing. Arthur would make me a steak or something for dinner, too. These brief reprieves from having nowhere to go were so important to me. Just knowing that there was one person left who still loved me and cared about me brought a tear of joy to my eye. After Arthur passed away, I found out that he had done these humble acts of charity for many people, never bragging about them or wanting any credit. There are so many kind, everyday people who reach out to their fellow human beings for no reason other that their conscience is telling them it's the right thing to do, and that's the kind of thing that can give you hope, even in your darkest hour.

When an old buddy wasn't there to help—and that was most nights, believe me—I would have to find somewhere else to rest my head. I slept in my car, of course, but the question was, where do I *park* the car so that I don't get hurt, robbed, or killed? The windows had to be left down because of how hot it usually was, which meant anyone could reach through them and do whatever they wanted. I often slept, or tried to sleep, under the bright, high lights of a shopping center parking lot. Between those lights shining down on me and the often sweltering heat, it wasn't what you'd call pleasant or restful, but at least I knew that it was highly unlikely some guy would jump out of the shadows, walk across that big parking lot, and assault me in an area where anyone could see his crime. It only takes a short period of being homeless before you find yourself constantly trying to avoid, outwit, or simply stay one step ahead of all the reprobates in your new world. So you park in your safe place and eventually the cops come along and shoo you away, and you're right back where you started.

My contact with Karen was pretty sporadic during this time. If there was some big news about Woody, she'd try to contact me, and I would try to call my son as often as I could. Who didn't I call? My old teammates. Never. Never, never, never. They and the other friends I'd made in my youth were lost to me. And I sure wasn't making any new friends on the streets. I didn't have that "the gang's all here" kind of addiction. Not the fun kind where you're all passing a bong around the frat house, and not the scary kind where you're all huddled around a crack pipe in a dilapidated, deserted house. There were no rituals to share with others. My addiction was solitary, and my days were spent alone, though I interacted with many people throughout each day in my exhausting, never-ending search for drugs. The "highs" didn't even feel like highs anymore; I now had to take an endless amount of pharmaceuticals just to "get to normal" and stop the cravings. Talk about anti-climactic.

If I had taken advantage of certain programs offered by both the government and church organizations, I would have never have had to be homeless, but for a long time, I just refused. It wasn't "me." In my drug-addled brain, it somehow seemed more dignified to live in a car and practice petty thievery against big corporations than to "take handouts" from Uncle Sam or crusading do-gooders. Sure, it was illegal, but it's not like I was holding people up with a gun or burglarizing homes. I had seriously thought of robbing a bank, but quickly dismissed the notion when a street acquaintance pointed out that my girth would be both an impediment to the getaway and an easy identifier. Heck, I wasn't even dealing drugs. The only time I'd ever done that was in Hilton Head, so very long ago, back when I was Mr. Popularity. Imagine what all those rich folks on the island would think of me now. Imagine what my late father-in-law, Woody Baldus, would have said about it. Would he have gotten angry with me, or just shaken his head sadly like all the other people I knew from my "old life"?

But even my twisted sense of pride couldn't last forever. After I broke into my ex-wife's house in 2005 and was arrested for it, a judge would not let me out of jail until I had a place to go, so I agreed to go to a homeless shelter called Fellowship House. I lived in their dormitories, ate their meals, and submitted myself to their rehab program. Everyone I met there, both men and women, had come from the same place as I did: the streets. There were hustlers, con men, drug dealers, prostitutes, burglars, robbers, beggars, you name it. Most of these shelters are not comfortable places, and since I had a shred of self-worth left—just a tiny one—I was almost happy that I did not feel comfortable there. Far too many of my fellow guests, however, did seem to feel comfortable at Fellowship House. Their dead eyes and hardened expressions told me that very few of them would ever escape the dreadful underworld that kept pulling them back in and spitting them back out into the shelters. It was a vicious cycle.

Upon graduating from the program at Fellowship House, I was given the opportunity to live in their low-cost housing, paying about $100 a week for a bare-bones apartment, and I took it. I even got a menial job from a temporary agency. But my attitude was still pretty crappy. I didn't like these kinds of programs. They were for losers who had never been pro football players or real estate wheeler-dealers. I didn't feel, deep down, that I was the kind of person who belonged in them, even though I was exactly the kind of person who belonged in them. One thing I never got all uppity about, though, was my appearance. It was worse than ever. I was so obese that not only did I avoid looking at my body in the mirror, I could hardly stand the sight of my face. So, in all this time on the streets—and even after they cleaned me up a little at the shelter—I never once went to any functions in proper society. No weddings, no awards ceremonies, no reunions, no funerals. Good thing no one really important in my life died during that period; I would have looked like an even bigger disgrace than I already did.

After holding my menial job down for a little while, I moved out of the Fellowship House apartments and into my former sister-in-law Kelly's apartment. (Don't ask me why these people kept giving me chance after chance—I don't know. They were saints.) I paid rent there, but started getting a little behind. Then I was arrested there on a Failure to Appear in Court charge. Since I had to stay in jail for about a week, I lost my job. My depression came raging back as I realized it was all starting again. Kelly couldn't put up with this forever. She'd have to kick me out soon, and I'd be back on the streets. There really was no hope. There really was no way out. I would just keep rolling and lying and playing my games until I wound up in prison or dead.

Then, around Thanksgiving of 2006, my ex-wife and my son came to me with an idea. Karen had printed out some information on a place called Canaan Land, and they wanted me to look it over. I didn't know much about the Bible at the time, but I knew that the word "Canaan" was in it, so that was enough for me to reject this place out of hand. I was a skeptic, like my dad. As far as I could see, God hadn't exactly been working overtime to fix my life. But when Karen told me that the guy who founded Canaan Land was an ex-biker, ex-drinker, and ex-heavy drug user, it piqued my curiosity. Still… Some one-year religious program? I couldn't even imagine myself in a place like that for a *week*, and I told her so.

"Maybe, then, you should talk to Woody about it," she said, and handed my son the phone before I could protest.

"Are you gonna go to Canaan Land, Dad?"

"I don't think so, Woody. After all I've been through, I just don't know if I can not see you for that long."

He was agitated. "Dad, you don't ever see me now, and when you do see me, you're not really there. I'm afraid you're going to die."

"Well, if I die, we'll see each other in heaven."

"Uh, no, you won't see me in heaven," Woody replied, "because you aren't going to *be* in heaven, Daddy." Touché. I was going to Canaan Land.

CHAPTER SIXTEEN

WHEN I MADE THE CALL to Canaan Land, I was informed, "We've got a six month waiting list."

I said, "Look, I can't wait six months. I don't think I'll be *alive* in six months."

The guy I was talking to—Phil Robertson, who I would soon come to know as a huge Alabama fan and love as a brother—said, "Well, let me think about it and pray about it. I'll get back to you." And he did get back to me: "I can get you in here on January 7th."

That meant it would be about another month before I could check in, which I felt I could handle. "Okay," I told him. "I'll be there."

In preparation for the big day, I moved back in with Karen and Woody. I was still popping my pills, of course, but a calm came over the three of us because we now at least had some kind of goal, some bit of hope. There was no fighting. In fact, I spent Christmas 2006 with the Baldus family in North Carolina and we had a wonderful holiday together. I didn't fool myself, though. I knew that I was approaching the toughest thing I'd ever do, and it was a challenge to fight the dread that constantly threatened to overtake me. This had to be done, and I was going to do it.

Karen drove me to Canaan Land when the time came, and as soon as we got there, I commenced freaking out. Canaan Land is in Autaugaville,

101

Alabama, and Autaugaville, Alabama, is in the middle of nowhere, with a population of about 870 people and a median income of about $23,000. When most Americans think of "rehab," they think of the tabloid tales of washed-up movie stars and former pro athletes getting some R&R at luxurious spas. Well, this former pro athlete didn't find himself in the lap of luxury, I'll tell you that. He found himself deep in the woods, and the first building he saw was an old, run-down lodge.

I walked up to the lodge and looked through one of the streaked windows, then turned to Karen and said, "Ain't no way I'm staying here."

She just rolled her eyes. "Well, you're not coming back with me, so..."

I heaved a sigh of relief when I saw a big, modern building over to our right, and was informed that I'd be living and working there, like everyone else at Canaan Land. The old lodge was just for storage.

Saying goodbye to Karen was emotional, but not emotional enough. Once you're divorced from someone and know it's truly over, you just aren't going to get the kind of romantic send-off that can tide you over for months and months. You must settle for platonic comfort, and look within yourself for all the strength it will take. I had taken my last Lortab (unknown to Karen) as we were en route to my new home, so any comfort from that would be a matter of mere hours.

After Karen left, they took me inside, where they did a full body search and went through all my stuff to look for drugs (there were none). I couldn't complain about the accommodations. I was assigned my own room, and though it was small (about 10x10), it was nice and clean, with a twin bed, a closet, and a desk for studying. In fact, the whole place was really nice, if a bit Spartan. There were big, comfy sofas in the communal area, and two weight rooms where we could work out. The kitchen and dining areas were as clean as a whistle. A guy named Heath sat me down in the office area and gave me an orientation/pep talk in which he told me that my life was about to change, that God loved me, and that I need not be afraid that I wasn't forgiven for the bad things I'd done in my life.

Meeting Heath, along with the head counselor, Joseph Wenrich, and the head director, Pastor Phil Bevilacqua, was a pleasant experience. Well, as pleasant as it could possibly be under the circumstances. Though they made it clear that I had screwed up my life and would have to change, they didn't come at me with pointless guilt-tripping and negativity. The people in charge at Canaan Land know that the men who come in for help have already beaten themselves up mentally and emotionally to the point where their self-esteem is almost nonexistent, and that the worst thing they can do is pile on. They stress the positive from the moment you walk in the door, telling you about all the guys they've known who came in just like you after hitting rock bottom, and how those guys are now leading completely different lives filled with joy, family, friends, and regained or newly-discovered faith.

And then I met Canaan Land's founder, Mac Gober. Mac had been through so much tragedy in his life: he had been physically abused as a boy by his father; he had served a nightmarish tour in Vietnam and suffered from Post-Traumatic Stress Disorder for years after; he had been in a hardcore motorcycle gang where violence was ubiquitous and life was cheap; and he had been a near-hopeless alcoholic and drug addict. No matter what kind of suffering or pain a man brought into Canaan Land, Mac could match it. He had been there. Yet he had totally turned his life around, and since 1981, he and his wife Sandra had been working through Canaan Land to do the same for others. The very first time I met Mac, he put his arm around me and said, "Hey, look, it's going to be okay. Things are going to be different. If you'll just follow what we teach, things will be okay." That was really important for me to believe, along with one of the first verses from Scripture I heard after checking in, Jeremiah 33:3: *Call unto me, and I will answer thee, and show thee great and mighty things, which thou knowest not.*

In the first two months of my stay at Canaan Land, I needed to remind myself of that verse over and over again, because physically speaking, it was hell. The cravings were terrible. With the flu-like symptoms and the aching joints, I was in a lot of *extreme* discomfort. Between the vomiting and the diarrhea, I was constantly running to the bathroom. Because of the stopped-up sinuses and the Restless Leg Syndrome, I could hardly sleep at night. For weeks on end, I was just a zombie, dragging myself around Canaan Land in the most miserable state I'd ever been in. And I was amazed that it wasn't like that for every addict at the center: Right from the start, I saw guys who came in on their last high, had a prayer said over them, and appeared to "get better" immediately. One heroin addict from New York City took his last shot on the bus, but never had another craving once he stepped foot on the property. I'm happy for them now, of course, but at the time, all I could think was, "Man, even when it comes to detoxing, I'm a total loser!"

My sickness didn't, however, stop me from appreciating the good old-fashioned southern food they put in front of me at every meal time. It had been so long, and the smell and taste of that fried chicken, those buttermilk biscuits, and those gravy-slathered mashed potatoes sure did my heart good. Closing my eyes and inhaling, I might as well have been back at Mrs. Wilkes' Dining Room in Savannah. And any southerner will know what was running through my subconscious: *Someone actually loves me.* Food has always equaled love to us. Sure, I may have dashed to the bathroom and puked it all up right away, but it's the thought that counts.

The folks who ran Canaan Land did love me, but man, were they strict with the rules and regulations. It's not easy for a mentally unstable person who is coming off drugs to know that he *has* to go Bible study every morning, *has* to work every afternoon, *has* to do this and that in exactly the way he's told to do them. The stress was overwhelming, and at times I felt like I was having a total nervous breakdown. I just wanted to run, but there was nowhere to run to, thank God. I was out in the boondocks, not even within walking distance of a main thoroughfare, and that was right where I was staying. Oh, people could—and did—leave Canaan Land at times. They'd drive you to a bus stop if you asked them to. But I didn't even have enough money to buy a bus ticket. I had nothing but the clothes on my back. For a while, that seemed like a curse, but I slowly came to understand that it was really a blessing in disguise. It kept me in the place I needed to be.

I'm sure it won't be a surprise to you that even as the drug cravings slowly left my body, my rebellious nature didn't just suddenly pick up and leave with them. There were times in those early days when I became very angry with the staff at Canaan Land, though my battles were always verbal, never physical. I wasn't too happy about having to take orders from counselors who were young enough to be my children, but age aside, they were a lot farther along on their journey than I was. They weren't going to let me B.S. them and they weren't going to change the rules for me, no matter how much of my father's debating skill I had inherited. Still, I gave it the old college try, questioning this, that, and the other thing until I was blue in the face. All I got for my trouble were essay-writing assignments of up to 10,000 words. Yeah, lots of fun.

Slowly, slowly I learned to stop questioning and arguing and just do what I had to do. Like everyone else, I'd get up at 5:00 AM, make my bed and clean my room, before heading to the dining room for breakfast. Then I'd go to "praise and worship" for an hour, which was lots of praying and music. After that, I'd sit through three hours of Bible classes. Then I'd have lunch and spend the afternoon working whatever job they assigned me. The "working" part of my day was actually the easiest part of it. At least if my muscles were aching and my legs were doing their crazy dance, I could move around and stretch a bit. But sitting for hours in worship and classes was very hard for me in the beginning. My mind raced and my body rebelled, and knowing that months and months of this stretched before me was mental torture. What had I gotten myself into?

I now realize that the work schedule was about a lot more than stretching my still-obese body. Attendance at Canaan Land is free to all who go there, and Mac Gober, his staff, and their biggest supporters work their hearts out to keep it that way. But they can't do it alone; they need the labor of its students to keep going. And for an alcoholic, a drug addict, a homeless person, or a criminal to be told "We *need* you" is a huge psychological boost. He is used to being thrown away, discarded, dismissed as a menace to society. The work might seem menial and pointless at first, but as the weeks and months go on, he realizes that even sweeping a floor or scrubbing a pot can be a baby step in the direction of regaining his dignity.

Though the phrase "fake it 'til you make it" perfectly describes my first few months at Canaan Land, I did pray in solitude as well, or tried to. At first I just begged God to take the cravings away and heal my aching body. But then, slowly, I began praying for other things: the restoration of my relationships with family and friends, a return to the normality I had known so briefly and loved so much, and the ability to lay my head down at night and sleep peacefully. Guilt and fear still ruled my life, but at least I was observing others who had overcome these demons—and starting to believe that it could happen for me, too.

CHAPTER SEVENTEEN

IT WAS EASY TO FOR ME to make friends at Canaan Land. All of us had the same kinds of problems, and most of us were ready to open up and talk about it. We were there in a last-ditch effort to save our lives, and we leaned on one another for support. Though some of us were criminals, the crimes were mostly things like petty drug dealing and public intoxication. Don't think I'm defending such behavior; I'm just letting you know why I wasn't afraid to reach out to my fellow patients. It's not like I was forced to live with violent felons or child molesters. Though we were all messed-up human beings, I felt safe and comfortable at Canaan Land, and as I slowly shed my drug cravings and paranoia, that secure feeling grew and grew.

But though our isolation was a great comfort in some ways, at other times it could feel restrictive and controlling, because it was *supposed* to feel restrictive and controlling. We could not read newspapers or watch TV. I didn't see a news program for fifteen months and had no idea what was going on in the outside world. Movies on DVD were allowed, but they had to be approved by the staff, and that meant a G rating. We weren't crazy about that, but at least it was some kind of diversion. On the weekends we were allowed to watch football or whatever other sport was in season, and that was a big treat, but a counselor was always in control of the remote.

We'd play cards and checkers or lift weights indoors, or go outdoors and shoot some hoops or fish in the nearby lake. On rare occasions, they would take us on a day outing to see a film at a movie theater, but again, only if they could find something "decent." So it was all quite bearable, but it was never really fun. The seriousness of our situation was always foremost in our minds.

To keep up that level of seriousness, every weekday afternoon we worked hard. We made food in the kitchen. We cleaned the interior of the center. We did lawn work around the buildings. Some guys worked in an automotive shop they'd set up on the property, which was a great way to explore a new trade. The type of work you did really wasn't important; the point was to just get you on a schedule and in the right frame of mind. One had a responsibility to work for his daily bread, though he also had an obligation to share it with those less fortunate. That might seem so simple and obvious, but if a guy's been living outside the boundaries of "normal" society for months, years, or even decades, he has to be re-taught even the most basic standards of civility.

I'll give you an example: Little Bill (as opposed to Big Bill, who was You-Know-Who) was in his fifties and had been on the streets for many, many years in Colorado. This tiny man broke our hearts, because he had forgotten everything about living as a self-respecting human being. When he washed himself in the communal shower, he would drop his filthy clothes at the shower door, then snatch them back up on the way out and put them right back on his body. He had no understanding of "changing clothes," because he'd only had one set of clothing for a very long time. He'd come in from working outside and lie down on his bed with those nasty clothes still on. We had to very gently guide him into the proper hygiene. And his problems went beyond the exterior: He needed guidance in regards to polite conversation, and his illiteracy made the memorization of Bible verses a frustrating experience. Though Little Bill could really be a pain in the butt, I came to love the guy, and I'm happy to report that the last I heard, he went back to Colorado a changed man and is doing well in his new life.

Every Friday, we students at Canaan Land were allowed to make one fifteen-minute phone call, but only if we had memorized and could recite three verses from scripture (and hadn't gotten into any trouble that week).

My call was always to Karen and Woody. During those calls, I tried very hard to keep a positive attitude and not upset my ex-wife, but it wasn't easy. And memorizing scripture wasn't always easy either; I missed a few phone calls and didn't like that one bit. But slowly, the verses I heard every day were beginning to speak to me, some reminding me of my biggest failures. *Ephesians 5:25: Husbands, love your wives, even as Christ also loved the church, and gave himself for her.* Well, I'd sure dropped the ball on that one, hadn't I? I had checked out of my marriage emotionally when I fell back into drug addiction, then left Karen to raise our son on her own. I needed to learn to love and respect that woman, even if we were now divorced. *Isaiah 54:13: And all thy children shall be taught of the Lord; and great shall be the peace of thy children.* Poor Woody had only known peace in the first five or six years of his life; after that he was forced to witness his father's slow descent into madness and his parents' constant fighting. I had to dedicate my remaining years to repairing the damage I had inflicted on my son. I found the hope that I could accomplish these things in other verses, verses that told me I could put my despair and self-loathing behind me. *Psalms 23:4: I will fear no evil, for thou art with me, Lord. Your word and your spirit, they comfort me.*

I hadn't felt comfort in a long, long time, but now I was starting to know it, and to trust it. Sometimes we would leave Canaan Land to go on luxury bus trips to Christian events or—once a year—a Florida vacation, but every time we returned to the center, a feeling of peace and contentment washed over me. When I heard about other guys who had left the program, it only reinforced my will to soldier on and see this thing through. I no longer wanted to run, to flee. Canaan Land may have only been a temporary home, but it was a home, and I knew it would teach me what I needed to know to once again have my own home in the "real world."

I was seeing miraculous changes in some of the men around me, especially the ones I was closest to. Conrad had been a court stenographer in Georgia before he lost everything to drugs, just like I had. He was a good ol' boy whose addictions had made him self-absorbed and cold, but at Canaan Land, he learned to open up and start truly caring about those around him. When my first Christmas time at the center rolled around, Conrad saw how down in the dumps I was about not being able to buy a present for Woody. Rather than just patting me on the back and telling me it would all be okay, he took up a collection from all the students and staff and gave me that money so that I could buy something for my son. I'll never forget that.

Another good friend I made at Canaan Land was Chris, a black guy from Tampa who had been in prison for drugs. Chris knew what a hard road he had to take to get back to some semblance of normality. Even in this day and age, his race would be an extra strike against him. But he was determined to do it, and he wasn't the least bit bitter about it. He cared just as much about my problems as he did his own, and our discussions about our fears, struggles, and goals for the future were really important to me.

I made friends with some of the staff, too. One of the teachers, Zach, had a really great sense of humor, and he kept my spirits up when times got tough. His personality also convinced me that becoming a Christian wouldn't turn me into some dead-serious, puritanical bore. It was okay to feel joy at God's goodness. It was okay to laugh and sing and clap and dance. Though I had pretended to convert several times before, part of the reason it never "took" was that I thought I couldn't behave the way I assumed other Christians did. It seemed like a big drag, having to dress all spiffy and watch every word that came out of your mouth. But as I saw other guys come into Canaan Land, and how they were welcomed by the staff, and how fellow patients greeted them by setting gifts of clothing and toiletries on their beds, I realized that the whole point was to come as you are. Christ already knew all your sins, and there was no need to hide your true identity.

Supporters on the outside were such a big boost, too. Because of my obesity, clothing was a challenging issue for me right from the start. But a terrific couple from Minnesota, the Larsons, bought me a wardrobe of clothes to replace the nasty rags I came in with. Because of the extreme isolation at Canaan Land, contact with outsiders like the Larsons was so meaningful. It was like someone was telling you, "Hey, you're not going to be thrown back into society with no support. You're part of a community now, and we are looking forward to the time when you're ready to join us." A simple, kind gesture like a gift of clothing can make you believe that someday, you'll be ready to live up to the faith these people are putting in you.

I was supposed to graduate from the Canaan Land program after twelve months, but as I neared that date, founder Mac Gober called me into his office and said, "I'm not going to let you graduate." I was shocked and devastated. What did these people want? Hadn't I done everything they'd asked me to do? Hadn't I immersed myself in the Bible classes and memorized a ton of scripture? Hadn't I changed my attitude and reached out to students and staff with an open mind and an open heart? I thought of all the times I'd been expected to swallow my pride, like when I'd arrived back at the center a few minutes late after a visit with Woody and they'd chewed me out. Seemed like even when I tried to do the right things, like rebuilding my relationship with my son, they'd find something to pick at. Well, that time I had just lost it, and now I felt I was being judged on those rare outbursts rather then the good behavior I displayed on most days. As I sat there and seethed, Mac added, "Now, you can stay, and graduate when I think you're ready, or you can pack up and leave."

Mac knew what he was doing. He knew me well enough by then to know that if he challenged me, I wasn't going to back down. After thinking about what he'd said for a few hours, I went back to his office and told him, "I'm not letting you run me off. I'm gonna finish this thing if it kills me. I haven't finished anything in a long time, and I need to finish this." So, they loaded me down with a bunch of teaching CDs, and I took matters into my own hands, studying for many additional hours after my regular classes each day and writing essay after essay about what I was learning. It turned out to be a period of real awakening and growth for me, and I can now look back and say that I am so happy I stuck it out. After an additional three months, Mac informed that I had made it: I would be graduating from Canaan Land.

For the first time in so long, I had actually accomplished something, and it was something that was far beyond a sports honor or a real estate deal. I was entering a new life, and I was more than ready to live it.

CHAPTER EIGHTEEN

AFTER I GRADUATED in April of 2008, I didn't just up and leave Canaan Land. Instead, I stayed on and became a counselor myself. What were my qualifications? Surely not that I was some learned ·biblical scholar. My theology was fairly simple and I'd be the first to admit that I had—and still do have—plenty more to learn, but I thought I was a good example of what could happen to guys who applied themselves and worked hard at the program. My street sense and my degree from the School of Hard Knocks meant that new students couldn't just come in and pull the wool over my eyes; I'd been there and I'd tried the same crap. I knew how much of my change was the result of seeing others who had gone before me, and now I wanted to be an example for others, too.

Mac Gober and others on the staff taught me to approach these incoming patients at their own level, and offer them unconditional love. They told me that I should never be surprised when drug addicts act like drug addicts or alcoholics act like alcoholics. In fact, it was important to *expect* that behavior and to know how to respond to it. When a new guy got frustrated or had a meltdown, we counselors were to keep calm and exhibit endless patience. It wasn't easy, but this practice is so beneficial, because it winds up teaching the teacher as much as the student. Ministering to the students was a constant reminder that faith is about so much more than one moment of "born again" ecstasy. No, faith is like working out: If you don't work on it all the time, it's going to get weak. But if you hold fast and just keep plowing through the work, your faith will grow.

I saw some miraculous changes in some of the guys I worked with, and it was so satisfying to think that I might have had even a tiny role in their transformations, but I'm not going to try to convince you that I had suddenly become some spiritual superman who could convince anybody to follow the same road I had. Some of these "kids" were hardcore addicts or almost lifetime victims of homelessness and family dysfunction. One day I was checking a new guy in, and I had to confiscate several pocket knives that were in his bag. I was, of course, concerned that he would harm someone else with them, but when I questioned him about it, I realized that my concern was misdirected: He pulled up his shirt and I was shocked to see row after row of scars running across his chest and abdomen. This was how this kid had been relieving his unbearable stress.

I also remember a young guy named Nathan. Timid, shy, and strange, he could hardly look us in the eye or speak to us as we were admitting him. It was hard for me to relate to him, because he was so introverted—the exact opposite of what I had been at that age. I tried to reach out to him and bond over our shared experiences with substance abuse, but I just don't think I ever got through to him. I know he felt like he was worthless, and I hate to think of what had happened in his life to make him feel that way. But sometimes you just have to admit that you don't have all the answers for every single patient, and simply leave it in the hands of God. I'll always wonder what happened to Nathan.

We counselors also learned a lot through working with each other. If the director saw two guys who didn't get along, he'd often purposefully put them together on a day-to-day basis and force them to work on the same projects. This was to prepare us for what we would face when we finally got out. It wouldn't be "nothing but unconditional love" when we were back out there looking for jobs and places to live. We had to learn how to get along with all kinds of different people, and how to respond to adversity with cool heads and calm hearts. This practice of pairing off opposing personalities led to me making a lot of friendships I never would have expected, with a lot of people I *thought* I had nothing in common with. I realized that there were times when I should apologize to my coworkers, even when I felt I was not wrong, just to cut the tension and start again with a new slate. That was something I thought I would never do.

As I became more confident in my position inside the center, the people in charge put more trust in me as far as outside activities. I was allowed to do things like go into town and do a little shopping, or to go to a doctor's appointment (unfortunately, my health problems were as bad as ever), or to drive students to their GED classes, as long as I was accompanied by another staff member. Then I was allowed "overnights" with Woody (who was a little baffled by the changes in me, to be honest). Then I began speaking at local churches and even gave an interview to a local television station. Though I still felt judged for being overweight (I'll address that later), what I was feeling *inside* was coming through loud and clear, and everyone could recognize it. The support from my brothers at the center was wonderful. They assured me I was going to be a blessing to many people. Mac Gober even told me that someday I would write a book about my journey. I just kind of chuckled and said, "Well, that would be nice, but I don't think it's going to happen."

Although there was a lot of support for me at Canaan Land, there was also a lot of concern. Spiritually, I was making great progress, but physically, I was still a mess. I'd been to the hospital for chest pains and those never-ending kidney stones, and my knees were destroyed because of the weight they'd been carrying. I could hardly even walk. Once we went to a conference at the civic center in Birmingham, and boy, was that an eye-opening experience. They parked the bus way out in this parking lot, and we had to walk quite far to get to the building. Sweat was just pouring off me, and I had to keep sitting down on benches and resting. I was freaking out and thinking, *"What on earth is going on? Can I really not even make it across a parking lot anymore?"* Soon after this scary situation, Pastor Phil called me into his office and said, "Look, I'm really worried about your health. You're going through a rigorous spiritual growth program, but I'm afraid you're going to drop dead while you're here. I want you to work out for a certain amount of time every day."

I started lifting weights again in the Canaan Land weight room. I had forgotten how much I loved working out. I also cut back a bit on my portions at mealtime, and I did lose a little weight. But "a little weight" was just not going to be enough, and I knew it. What was happening to me on the inside was making me want to take care of the outside, too. It may sound cliché to say, "My body is a temple," but I was truly coming to believe it. So... where to start? I decided to end the half-hearted attempts and throw my whole life into this thing: I sent in an application and an audition tape to the television show *The Biggest Loser*. The producers of that show invited me to a Nashville casting call, and they interviewed me there on camera. Unfortunately, this time around they were casting couples and people with partners, so they had to give me a pass. But one of the casting people said, "Do you mind if I submit your name to some other similar shows that are casting? I believe you'll be selected for one of them if I do. Your story's a good story and your weight definitely makes you a candidate for it." I of course responded positively, and a few months later she called me and said, "There's a show called *Heavy* coming out on A&E; we're casting for it right now, and I'd like to come down and film an interview with you."

I was amazed at how much time and work goes into casting these reality weight-loss shows. They came to Alabama and interviewed me, my ex-wife, and my son on camera. They did exhaustive question-and-answer sessions with me in which they asked about everything from my daily routine to my sex life. I guess when I heard the phrase "television producers" I had expected to be dealing with gray-haired old men, but the producers of *Heavy*, Erin Flinn and Lyndsey Burr, were relatively young women. I loved their energy and their positive attitudes; I knew right from the start that these were people I'd enjoy working with (and to this day, I stay in touch with Erin and Lyndsey). Sure, it was a little humiliating to reveal my innermost secrets, but I had a really good feeling that there would be a transformation that would make it all worth it. Throughout this time I had been praying, "If I'm not doing the right thing here, if I'm just wasting my time, let me know. Let me get a feeling." I felt those prayers were answered when the casting people kept reassuring me, "Don't worry, it'll happen. It's just a matter of the right show at the right time." And sure enough, a producer of *Heavy* called me in March 2010 and said, "Congratulations—you've been selected for *Heavy!*"

I had already told the Canaan Land staff that I'd be leaving in May, so I was thrilled to find out that the show would begin filming on May 4. To me, it was just one more sign that none of this was coincidental; it was part of God's plan for me. I'd make about $5,000 doing the show, which was more money than I'd seen in ages. But I was even more happy that the show would be filmed at a beautiful weight-loss center on a place that had been so important in my life—Hilton Head Island. Wow: 5,000 bucks and a six-month, rent-free stay on Hilton Head! That was my idea of a weight-loss plan. When I told everyone at Canaan Land the details, they were unanimously supportive.

Just as touching was the support I got from a men's group at a local church. I had given a speech there in which I'd told them about selling my National Championship rings for dope, so when I announced that I'd gotten the space on *Heavy* and came to say goodbye to them, they presented me with a replacement for one of those rings. They had to go through the NCAA and the U. of A. to do it, so my heart was about ready to burst when they gave it to me. It was a very emotional parting, but I knew these new friends and I would still be together in spirit.

Finally, the day came to leave Canaan Land. The producers of *Heavy* had rented me a car, and off I went, traveling that old path to Hilton Head as a new man. It was so strange to be able to choose my speed, take whatever route I wanted to take, and stop the car whenever and wherever I wanted to stop it. It was like, *"Look at me—I'm pumping gas and buying food at a BP all by myself! I'm a real grown-up again!"* I drove on and on, so confident and so excited, and then I saw that long, familiar bridge and my beautiful island. There was no better place to start righting all the wrongs.

CHAPTER NINETEEN

THAT FIRST NIGHT ON HILTON HEAD, the show put me up in a hotel and I had dinner with my ex-mother-in-law, Kathy Baldus, who was there for the summer. It meant a lot to me that Kathy was still in my corner after all I'd put her and her family through. We had a great time together, and the next morning I checked into the Hilton Head Health Institute, where *Heavy* would be filming.

The Institute usually charges clients about $3,300 a week for their services, so I felt really lucky to be there at no cost. I had always heard about how exclusive it was and all the mega-rich people who went there to lose weight. Everyone was so nice and welcoming, and I couldn't believe it when I saw the very first person to greet me: Bob Wright. Bob had been a friend of one my roommates from my wild years on Hilton Head and was now an executive at the Institute. I don't know who was more shocked when we laid eyes on one another: me or him. I also don't know what shocked Bob more: the way I looked, or simply the fact that I was back on the island. He had certainly known my reputation, and why I'd had to flee all those years before.

It didn't bother me one bit that a camera was on me from the second I pulled into the place. I loved the attention. They filmed me checking in and saying hello to everyone, but of course that was all for show, because all the paperwork had been completed long before. They didn't have everyone in the cast come in at the same time; they admitted us one by one over a few days so that they could film us individually and take their time. We kind of trickled in slowly. The first fellow cast member I met was a woman named Sallie from Gulf Shores, Alabama. She was a huge Alabama fan. HUGE. Like, so huge that I gave her my National Championship ring to wear the first day, and that nearly drove her crazy with excitement. Sallie and I became instant friends, and we shared something right off the bat: We both weighed in at 443 lbs.

Two people from the cast would be featured in each episode, and shortly after we'd all arrived, they told us who our episode partner would be. Mine was Julia, a woman who had become obsessed with food and eating while nursing her terminally ill mother. When the cameras weren't around, Julia and I pretty much did our own things, but not because there was any animosity there or anything. We just didn't have all that much in common. I had a lot of respect for her, though, because she took her time at the Institute seriously and lost 94 lbs. She had a good work ethic and inspired those around her to work as hard as she did. But then, everyone in the cast had a great attitude. I was proud to be on the show with all of them.

The producers put us up in some really nice condos, and I shared mine with a male roommate. It was like a vacation rental, and it never ceased to amaze me that I was living there rent free, with no worries about bills. I had a king-sized bed, a flat-screen TV, my own bathroom, and all the freedom in the world in the evenings. They even provided us with all the "little things", like toiletries. It felt so luxurious to be there immediately after leaving the austere environment at Canaan Land, where I had lived in a tiny room with a tiny bed and no TV. Whereas a lot of my cast mates were coming from a regular lifestyle and regular houses and felt like they were being put in a prison, I felt like I was being *released* from a prison. I figured whatever I'd have to do there at the Institute would almost be a cake walk compared to the rigorous program at Canaan Land, so I was in heaven.

Almost a cake walk, but not quite. The first few days, especially, were just incredibly intense. We were immediately put on a very strict, approximately 1200-calorie-a-day diet, and I was starving. *Starving*. The first night we were there, they served us steak, and I remember thinking, "Uh, did you *drop* part of this steak?" We were only allowed four ounces of any kind of meat. That was a lot less than I was used to eating. The meat would be accompanied by steamed vegetables devoid of anything fun like butter or salt, and salads with very lo-cal dressings—no ranch or anything like that. Come on, now! Depriving an American male of his ranch dressing? That's cruel and unusual punishment. But the torture was carried out in a beautiful dining room, and it all felt so "five star." We sat down together for every meal and were served by the type of waiters you'd expect to find working in a high-end hotel.

The calorie amount was posted on every meal, so you knew exactly how much you were taking in. Our weight-loss counselors preached "low fat, high protein, low carb," but in practice, it all seemed to come down to portion control. Calories in, calories out. I've found in my time since being there that I can eat almost anything I want, as long as I control my portions. So, if I'm trying to stick to 2,500 calories per day and I eat a candy bar or some other "bad" food, it just means I have to eat a little less for the rest of the day and make sure I do an appropriate amount of exercise. Now, burning those calories off with a workout is one thing when you're simply trying to maintain your weight, but at the Institute, when I was trying to lose weight, it was obviously a lot more difficult. Burning 1,000 or 2,000 calories a day is no walk in the park. It's rough.

The cameras were on us constantly for those first few days, and they threw us into the exercise just like they threw us into the diet: suddenly and forcefully. The bikes and the treadmills were lined up and ready to go, but I was not so ready to go. My spirit was all in, but my body was another matter. My knees were so shot that all I could do at first was ride a recumbent bike for four or five minutes, then rest for a bit, then do four or five minutes more, then rest for a bit. I didn't get down about that, though. I had known it would be that way in the beginning. Then they put us in a boxing class and instructed us to punch a padded wall. That was about as close as I came to passing out that first day, and I realized they were pushing us as hard as they could to get some good "impact" scenes on camera. Man, were we in awful shape.

I do believe that the workouts were initially easier for me than they were for many of my cast mates, though, and the reason for that was obvious: It may have been a long time since I'd exercised seriously, but because of my athletic past, I knew what to expect. You don't forget the kind of grueling workouts you did in the Alabama football program or the NFL, no matter how many years have passed. I understood how hard this was going to be and how much pain I'd be in, and I had mentally prepared myself for it. Some of the other cast members, however, had never exercised in their lives. Never. You could see the shock and fear in their eyes for those first few days. It was just overwhelming for them, and I did what I could to reassure them that it would get better. We had a meeting one day soon after arriving, and I stressed the importance of not letting up on the intensity. They needed to sustain it for the whole six months, I told them, not just be happy with *some* weight loss and then slack off after a few months. I felt like I really got through to them, and I have to say that aside from a tiny bit of goofing off in the last few weeks, they heeded my warning. My cast mates all managed to hang tough, and I found that really admirable.

I got into a rhythm very quickly and pretty much did the same thing every day, day after day. I'd walk or ride a bike to the Institute every morning and have my 200- or 300-calorie breakfast, which was served buffet style. Then I'd get on a recumbent bike for about an hour, and after resting for about ten minutes, I'd do 45 minutes or so of some other kind of cardio. After lunch, I'd do two more exercise classes. Then dinner, then home to my condo. The workouts may have been overwhelming at first, but I was surprised at how quickly my body adapted. The human body really is an amazing thing, the way it can recover from the most awful abuse. Soon, I was craving even more exercise than we did during the day, and I used the freedom they gave us at night to exceed their requirements. I'd take my bike and ride along the moonlit beach, or take a long, long walk or run in the sand. This was a great stress reliever, a wonderful time to meditate on where I'd been and pray about where I was going. *"God, let me represent You well, let me represent my family well, let me represent Alabama well. But most of all, You."*

Whenever the producers and camera people came to visit—which was not all that often—they would film us weighing in and working out, and then do our individual interviews. The interviews were filmed outdoors, with the beautiful palm trees and hanging moss of Hilton Head as a background. Sometimes these question-and-answer sessions could go on for an hour or more, but I didn't mind. I'd delve deeply into my pain and loss, and by the end it was not unusual for me, the female producer who was interviewing me, and the male cameramen to all be in tears. They didn't mind if I talked about my faith, but I knew a lot of that would be cut. First of all, I was under no illusions about the type of TV show this was: It was a secular show about weight loss, not a Christian show about faith. Second of all, an "hour-long" show is really only about 40-42 minutes without commercials, and each episode of *Heavy* featured two cast members. So, that's what? About 20 minutes of airtime each? You have to have realistic expectations.

Speaking of reality, I could take comfort in the fact that even if *Heavy* was not a vehicle for evangelism, it was at least an inspirational show that was clean and safe to watch for viewers of all ages. It was one of those "classy" reality shows that were part of a backlash against reality shows that were... well, not so classy. Yes, they wanted drama, but they wanted nice, wholesome, uplifting drama in an upper-class environment. There weren't going to be any messy, drunken confrontations. No one was going to start screaming and pulling out hair extensions. I didn't have to worry that a half-naked Kardashian or a five-year-old beauty pageant queen would wander into the shot while I was being interviewed. I just decided to keep my eyes on the big picture and be thankful for all the great stuff about the show, and all the wonderful people I was meeting. And, uh, to thank God that reality TV had not been around when I was in my twenties.

CHAPTER TWENTY

A S THE MONTHS AT THE INSTITUTE went on, I became closer and closer to my cast mates from *Heavy*, but also to the "regular" clients there. We had long, long discussions about our lives and the issues that had brought us to this place. I didn't mind opening up and getting personal, because everyone else was doing the same and showed so much compassion for what I'd been through. I always tried to return that compassion when they told their stories. There was the woman who had started overeating when her dad committed suicide. The woman who was chowing her way through a rough marriage. The kid (well, he was twenty years old, but he seemed like a "kid" to me) who had been adopted and was searching for his biological family. The woman who had never been held or loved by a man in her life. The "little person" whose dwarfism combined with a weight problem to cause him all kinds of health problems. And perhaps most tragically of all, the guy who had been in the army and lost everyone in his platoon to a firefight; he was the only one who made it out of there alive and was suffering from survivors' guilt.

Everybody at the Institute had a story like that. It was so good for me to hear them because it made me realize, after all that time at Canaan Land, that homeless people and drug addicts didn't have a corner on pain. You could be a high-flying member of the upper class, but if your mental, emotional, or physical health was ruined, forget about it. All the money in the world wasn't going to make up for that. Soon after I got to the Institute, one of the cast members clients collapsed on the floor and, knowing about my faith, he asked me to come over to him and pray with him. The paying clients witnessed this, and they soon asked me if we could have a little church service in one of the meeting rooms. We went in there and had a long talk and prayed for a guy who had gotten sick. I didn't have to (nor did I want to) shove my beliefs down anyone's throat; I simply stated them in a matter-of-fact way and allowed people to come to me if they felt the need. *Heavy* didn't hire a preacher; they hired a reality show guy, and I think I found a good middle ground that everyone was comfortable with.

Things weren't all sunshine and lollipops every day, of course; we were all tired and hungry and that combination can sure make you cranky. But we also understood that we were all good people just trying to survive, so we really made an effort to keep the clashes to a minimum. We'd razz each other to cut the tension. One young guy, Johnny, came into the Institute with a tattoo of a donut—with sprinkles!—on his arm. Now how could we possibly refrain from giving him the business about that? We'd tease the "girls," too, but those girls were grown women, and they'd give it right back to us. Keeping a sense of humor in a situation like that can really work wonders in the sanity department. Yes, we pushed each other in our workouts and didn't allow any slacking, but who says you can't tell a few jokes while you're sweating like a pig?

When the show was filming, we were required to do scheduled workouts with our episode partners, and it was usually stuff that looked more interesting, like boxing or Pilates. But when the cameras were gone, I could do it my way, as long as I did it. The Institute offered everything from strength training to yoga, and I might have tried those things if what I was doing hadn't been working, but it was working. I was concentrating almost 100% on cardio, because I was losing weight so quickly that I really didn't have the strength for weight training. Of course, the weight loss fluctuated. One week I lost 18 lbs.; another week I lost zero lbs. That didn't bother me (much), because I knew I was in it for the long haul. I was very conscious of not panicking, not overworking and burning myself out. And my excruciatingly painful knees were always there to remind me that I had to be careful about that. There were times when I'd have to sit in the dining room with huge bags of ice on both of them while I ate my meals. I took anti-inflammatory drugs before every workout. Finally, I wound up in an orthopedic surgeon's office for cortisone shots, and he told me that I'd never make it through the entire six months. But this is an example of why my rebellious streak is not always a bad thing; if I was told I couldn't make it, I was going to do it come hell or high water.

Whether the cameras were there or not, we were constantly monitored: weigh-ins, blood pressure, cholesterol, etc. I didn't mind that at all. It felt more caring than intrusive, because it was combined with regularly-scheduled strategy meetings with our coaches and counselors. We'd talk about working through the pain I was in, how to be very cautious about taking medicine during this process because of my addiction history, and how I could continue to be a motivating factor for the other people on the show. The staff was always so nice about telling me how much they appreciated my leadership qualities, and my cast mates did seem to respond well to my straightforwardness and honesty. Once again, I realized how important it was for me to stay on this path, and never return to my old life of lying to others and deluding myself.

Even if they hadn't been weighing us constantly, I would have known how successful I was from the fit of my clothing. Almost immediately, it felt like I was swimming in the clothes I'd brought to the Institute. I just kept pulling the belts and drawstrings tighter and tighter. Almost all I wore the whole time I was there was tee shirts and shorts, so it didn't really matter that everything was getting baggy. I just kept wearing it. Like most guys, I like baggy, casual clothes anyway, so it wasn't any big deal. Eventually, I got a smaller pair of crimson shorts with the Alabama "A" on them, and they reminded me of the Alabama Spring game I had attended right before I left to film *Heavy*. It had turned into a mini reunion between me and my former teammates and their spouses, and when I told them where I had been and what I had gone through, they were so supportive. To a person they had told me, "If you had called me during your time of crisis, I would have helped," and I know they meant it. It was so emotional when they sent me off with pats on the back and said things like, "Show 'em how Alabama does it."

I tried to keep those former teammates updated while I was on the show, and I was allowed to have contact with Karen and Woody, too. Woody was still kind of freaking out about the obvious changes in me. Sure, those changes were good, but they were so drastic that they were bound to be disturbing to a young person. Perhaps Woody thought that I would expect some kind of major and immediate lifestyle change in him, too. When I talked to him, I just tried to reassure him that what would be would be, that God was in control. I didn't want him to think that he had to do anything different to "win" my love; I told him that that love was unconditional and free. If we love the way Jesus loves, good things will happen all in good time; if we try to force God's hand, we will only wind up with a lot of frustration and disappointment.

I was amazed that my friends and family weren't the only ones who wanted to stay in touch about my progress. Someone made a Facebook fan page for me, which really blew my mind. Hey, I was sort of famous again, after so many years of not being sort of famous. The producers of *Heavy* talked to us about this social media stuff, telling us what we could and couldn't reveal when we talked to our fans online. Their biggest concern was that we not "spoil" the upcoming episodes by revealing how much weight we had lost. So, when I went to my Facebook fan page, I couldn't be specific and post something like, "I've lost 40 lbs. so far," but I could post something like, "Things are going well." And of course we were not allowed to post photographs, because that would clearly show our progress. I just loved talking to all these viewers online. They inspired me as much as I inspired them. And after all the restrictions on outside contact at Canaan Land, I felt as though I was slowly recovering some of the "adult" freedoms that normal people had in the regular world. I could "friend" whomever I wanted.

But just because I had the freedom to friend the whole world online, I knew that I had to be careful in my day-to-day life. How many times had I said I was going to change and then fallen right back into the same old dysfunctional ways? Well, I was determined not to let it happen this time. I knew that I had to associate with people who were going to support me in my new life, not fill me with doubt and negativity. That didn't mean that I was going to stop reaching out to the lost and the needy, but it did mean that I was going to make sure there were plenty of positive and uplifting people in my life, people I could call upon and talk to whenever that darkness threatened to overtake me again. That's why I was so happy to be on *Heavy*, and to still be in touch with my brothers at Canaan Land. These were all people who would encourage me to be the best I could be.

One day a week, we were allowed to leave the Institute and go to the movies. No, it wasn't easy, smelling that popcorn, but I spent as little time at the concession area as possible and stuck to Coke Zero. At the Institute itself, I drank almost nothing but water—tons of water, all day long. Once in a while, I'd have a cup of coffee. My food cravings got much better with time, as my body adjusted to its new routine. For the first month or so, I had really been missing cheeseburgers, fries, and other bad stuff, but I think I always craved quantity more than certain types of food. When you first begin using portion control, it just seems crazy, like you're starving yourself. But once you get into that mindset of burning off everything you eat—and more—you settle in both physically and mentally. Eventually I was able to satisfy my cravings with fruit, which was available to us pretty much 24 hours a day.

Another thing that changed as time went by were the spirits of my fellow cast members. I saw people who had been scared and unsure of themselves become strong and self-confident as they saw what they could accomplish. Not everyone lost 30 pounds in the first week, like one guy did. Others had more of a struggle on their hands, but they all rose to the occasion and did what they had to do, proving to themselves that they were stronger than they ever knew. We were all excited about being on TV and getting publicity, of course, but most of us realized that those things were just added benefits. Our lives were being saved, whether anyone was watching or not.

CHAPTER TWENTY-ONE

WHEN I SIGNED ONTO *Heavy*, I was—like most Americans—no longer under any illusions about reality TV. Not all reality shows indulge in blatant fakery; in the early years, on shows like *The Real World* (first broadcast in 1992) and *The Osbournes* (which began airing in 2002), it really did appear that the camera simply followed its subjects around and whatever happened, happened. But even back then, little "adjustments" were being made. When the terrorist attacks of September 11, 2001, occurred, the Chicago cast of *The Real World* was doing a photo shoot at Wrigley Field, and apparently the producers weren't happy with the reaction shots they got there. So they rushed the cast back to their communal apartment, plopped them down in front of the TV, and shot their "first reactions" there. Sure, they were upset and crying, but there was still some deceit involved.

As for the Osbournes, before they got the TV deal, Sharon Osbourne had always called her husband by his given name, John. Right from Episode One, however, she referred to him as "Ozzy," because the producers didn't want to confuse viewers. Imagine suddenly calling your spouse a different name after decades of marriage. But at least Sharon and Ozzy had a real relationship; the fake romances that ensued in later years on such shows as *The Millionaire* and *The Bachelor/Bachelorette* were laughably obvious and

131

embarrassing to watch. And the phoniness wasn't limited to romance; who can forget Johnny Fairplay lying about his grandmother's "death" on *Survivor*? Who can forget *Jersey Shore*'s JWoww wearing socks, then not wearing socks, then wearing socks again, as she watches a supposedly spontaneous fight between Snooki and Angelina? (Not that we all wouldn't *like* to forget those things.)

The anonymous editor of a reality TV show had this to say about his line of work on the website Buzzfeed: "The worst one I worked on in terms of manipulation was probably a dating competition show. That one basically just put some oversexed drunken kids in a house and let them go wild. Sometimes the producers would ask a contestant something like, 'What do you think about Steve? You don't like him?' And the contestant would say, 'No, I'm not going to say that I don't like Steve.' And the producers would ask us to cut everything except, 'I don't like Steve.'" The creator of *The Bachelor*, Mike Fleiss, went on record to defend his show, but criticized the genre nonetheless: "I think there's all kinds of (bull) going on behind the scenes, I would say, outside of the talent shows and *The Bachelor*, where we really kill ourselves and spend a lot of money and time and destroy our staff to make sure it's real, but 70 to 80 percent of the shows on TV are (bull). They're loosely scripted. Things are planted. Things are salted into the environment so events seem more shocking." Yet Fleiss insisted that it was no big deal to the viewers, adding, "They know it's somewhat fake, but they're OK with it."

My moment of reality "bull" on *Heavy* was shared with a staff member of the Institute who, for the purposes of this book, I will call "Natalie." My first meeting with Natalie seemed to go well. We discussed my case and the path I should take to weight loss, and everything was very calm and polite. But as time went on, Natalie's dislike of me became obvious. Many of my cast mates saw me as a leader of our group, so when controversies and complaints arose, they would ask me to go to the producers and/or the staff and represent us. None of the other authority figures had a problem with this, but Natalie did. She saw me as someone who stirred up the others and created problems that weren't really there. I don't feel I ever did that, but, as always, I was stubborn and refused to back down when I thought I and my cast mates were right.

Here is the interaction that *Heavy* viewers saw between Natalie and me: Natalie apparently questioning me in her office about my visit to an orthopedic doctor who prescribed me—Lortab. Me sitting there looking like a deer in the headlights. My son Woody giving me a strange look from across the room. Natalie staring and shaking her head at the both of us. Fast, choppy cuts as I looked at Woody, he looked me again, we looked at Natalie, Natalie looked at us, and absolutely nothing was resolved. All of this "action" was, of course, accompanied by dramatic music that screamed "life or death situation." The first time I saw this scene, I didn't know whether to laugh or cry. But enough time has gone by that it's definitely in the "laughing" category, and I'm glad I have chance to explain why.

There was so much that the viewers *didn't* see, and I'm not just talking about the contentious history between Natalie and me. Yes, I went to the orthopedic doctor because I was having excruciating knee pain. Yes, after having only limited success with cortisone shots, Tramadol (a non-narcotic drug), and some kind of prescription anti-inflammatory drug, he prescribed a low dose of Lortab, the drug that had once fed my raging addiction. But I was in constant communication with the staff at the Institute about the drugs he prescribed for me. I wasn't trying to hide anything, and even if I wanted to hide anything, it would have been impossible. Know why? Because a camera crew from *Heavy* followed me not just to the doctor's office, but right into the examining room!

After this examination, I went back to the Institute and immediately had a meeting with the head trainer and several other staff members. I told them every detail of what went on at the doctor's office. I asked for their advice and took it under consideration when I made the decision about which drug to take. *Everyone* knew *everything* that was going on at *every second.* There were no secrets. I didn't want any secrets. I just wanted to control this horrible pain so that I could continue working out and losing weight. Since everything was being filmed, I assumed viewers would see everything. Though I'd heard plenty about reality TV fakery, I still had no idea just how creative reality show editing could be.

So I took the Lortab for a short time, then stopped taking it and went back to taking only the anti-inflammatory stuff. But every time the show interviewed me, they kept bringing up Lortab and asking if I was still using it. Finally, I said, "Listen, I'm not going to let y'all turn this into a relapse. That's not what's going on, and you know that's not what's going on. I'm not going to talk about this anymore. Let's just finish what we're doing here." They let up on the subject, and I really didn't think that much about it until the show aired and I saw what they'd pieced together.

In our scenes together that were broadcast, Natalie was actually asking me about the anti-inflammatory drug I was taking. She asked me what it was called, and I couldn't remember its name. So I sat there looking like an idiot for a long, long minute while she rolled her eyes and expressed her disgust. But I know there wasn't one viewer out there who thought this question was about the anti-inflammatory drug. It looked like I was being queried about Lortab, and like I was stalling and lying. And doing all this in front of my young, innocent son, whom I had already hurt so much, so many times. (In reality, I had told Woody I was taking Lortab before he even got to Hilton Head, and had warned him about Natalie.)

Now, was it a risk for me to take any Lortab at all? Of course it was, but it was a risk I weighed carefully. The alternative risk was that I would have to quit working out, which meant I would have to quit the show and quit my dream of changing my weight and my life. It would be nice if all situations were black and white, and we always knew immediately which side to take, which choice to make. But life isn't like that. Even though I'd recently found a new faith, that didn't mean I suddenly had all the answers and was going to be a perfect role model for everyone watching the show. And frankly, I didn't want to try to pretend I was a perfect role model. I wanted to show myself for what I really was: a guy who was going to keep making mistakes, but who realized he had to face up to those mistakes and try to minimize the damage. That's the attitude I had throughout the entire show, but the editing of my scenes with Natalie made me look shifty and deceptive.

Who is to blame for all this? Certainly not just Natalie. While it's true that she didn't like me, and that she confronted me about a "problem" that really wasn't a problem (in my opinion), she didn't edit those scenes, and she didn't put them on air. The producers and editors of *Heavy* did that, and at first I wasn't too happy about it. But time has mellowed my opinion of the whole incident, and far from being angry about it, I'm more amused.

It's business. That is what they were hired for. That is their job. Yeah, they could have shown a more balanced report of what happened, and cut my scenes gently, and used a soothing rather than a disturbing soundtrack, but if they had, would my episode have been rated the highest to date? They had a former pro football player who was also a former addict on their hands, and they knew that making the most of that fact would boost their ratings. Do I find it hilarious that anyone would feel the need to exaggerate *my* life? Would anyone look at *my* life and say, "You know, we need a little more cray-cray here"? But that's today's "reality"; you can never be too dramatic or too crazy.

There are a lot of people who produce and edit a show like *Heavy*. I have no way of knowing who made this or that decision, who cut this or that scene, and who had the final say. And you know what? I'm glad I don't know, because most of my memories of actually making the show are positive ones—very positive. I consider all the people who worked on the show with me to be my friends and I am very thankful for the chance they gave me to change my body and my life. I want to be honest in this book, but I don't want to overemphasize the negative. Watching the final cut of the scenes with Natalie was just one small part of an experience that, overall, was one of the best of my life.

I know in my heart that I was honest with the show and with the staff at the Institute. I gave straightforward interviews and tried to get the truth out to the viewers, too. As I said at the beginning of this chapter, I went into this process with my eyes wide open, aware that reality TV was not always reality. That gives me hope that most of the people who watched my episode could see that facts were manipulated and that a ratings-grabbing story was patched together from a true story that just wasn't quite exciting enough for the suits at A&E. Hey, I'll be the first to admit it: Sober Bill is far less entertaining than Drug-Addicted Bill. Ask anyone who knows me in real life; they're all quite happy and relieved that I've stopped "entertaining" them. In a strange way, I guess it's actually a *good* thing that the show had to manufacture extra drama for me. At least I'm not still manufacturing it myself, right?

CHAPTER TWENTY-TWO

I STOPPED THINKING ABOUT the Lortab issue shortly after the incident with Natalie, but there was plenty of time to think about plenty of other subjects during my stay at the Institute, and of course one of those subjects was the current state of football culture in America. When you're an ex pro, people are constantly asking your opinion on football, and it was something I pondered regularly during my free time, especially at night as I walked, ran, or rode down the beautiful beach on Hilton Head. It's interesting to realize how some of your ideas have changed over the years, and hopefully evolved with the wisdom of age. Here are some of the issues I've been asked about over the years:

The Idolatry of Coaches and Football Programs

Let's address the elephant in the room right off the bat. When I left the Hilton Head Health Institute, the Jerry Sandusky scandal at Pennsylvania State University was still about a year away from busting wide open. But the problem that led to the cover-up was one I was aware of long before that: coaches and football programs being worshiped as gods. I had played under one of those "gods," Bear Bryant, for five years. However, I truly believe that Coach Bryant would never have thwarted an investigation of a serious crime like child molestation. Remember, this was a guy who punched a little hole in every shirt he wore so that he would never forget his humble roots. Fans may have worshiped him, but he didn't buy into it himself. He didn't see himself as above the law. Unfortunately, that's not true of all coaches, and it apparently was not true of Joe Paterno. Paterno thought he could take care of this mess himself on the downlow. I have no way of looking into his heart and knowing if he felt any guilt about the children whose lives were destroyed, but the bottom line is that he prevented them and their families from getting the justice they deserved.

What can be done to counteract this culture of idolatry and the out-of-control power that inevitably follows? In my opinion, coaches must be held accountable, just as players are. When players are caught committing crimes, their scholarships are oftentimes, and rightly, taken away. There should be some kind of review committee for coaches, and the coaching staff under them should be protected if they come forward with damaging information. We saw how intimidated the staff members at Penn State were; they were afraid of being blackballed not just at one university, but throughout the whole system. I'm not excusing their lack of courage, but I do understand how it happened. Communication is key in these situations, and they were too fearful of communicating with law enforcement authorities. That's just unacceptable, and hopefully something will be done to change it.

Are College Players Exploited?

This is a very complex issue. Players know going in that this is a business, and that colleges are going to make a lot of money off of them. They also know, in theory, that they are supposed to be getting an education at the same time that they're playing football. But one would have to be very naïve to believe that any coach is as enthusiastic about his players learning academic subjects as he is about them learning to be good football players. They are there to play football first, and if they happen to get a good education, too, that's fine. But it's not easy: Football takes up so much of these players' time that they have to put forth a huge effort to get something out of their studies and graduate with a worthwhile degree. And they certainly don't have time for a side job, so they often walk around without even enough money to go out on a date, put gas in their cars, or get their clothing dry cleaned. I find that ridiculous.

Is it so much to ask that these programs that are making millions and millions of dollars off these young people compensate them in some way? I don't care if it's pennies; if you're selling a jersey with a guy's name on it, at least show him enough respect to give him *something*. Am I really supposed to get all up in arms over something like the "tattoos-for-memorabilia" scandal at Ohio State? If we just admitted that what college players do is *work* and paid them to work, we wouldn't see this kind of petty corruption.

Are NFL Players Overpaid?

It's arguable, but one could make the argument that doctors and lawyers are overpaid, too. And here's the difference: Doctors and lawyers have a much longer time to practice their chosen professions. I really don't think most fans understand how short the average NFL career is: 6.86 years. And they also don't realize just how many hours a player puts in. You don't just show up on Sunday and play a game for four hours and go home. It is a full-time job, Monday through Sunday. And the off season has become a full time job, too; so much time and money go into individual training during those months. The off season is anything but a vacation. So, yes, NFL players are paid very well, but they work very hard for it and only get that kind of money for a very short time on average.

Is the NFL Doing Enough as far as Head Injuries?

It's hard for me to judge those at the top when it comes to this issue, because I know that for many years—many decades, actually—they had no idea what they were dealing with when it came to head injuries. But do I support the players who are suing the NFL over their head injuries? Absolutely. I have a friend in Alabama who is suffering from Lou Gehrig's disease, and his doctors are attributing it—at least partly—to the multiple concussions he endured during his playing time. And when I see a relatively young man like former Chicago Bears quarterback Jim McMahon struggling with early-onset dementia, well, it just freaks me out. As far as I know, I never had a concussion, but I easily could have, and I'm very grateful that they have a strong players union to fight for better retirement benefits and medical care.

Look, it's a violent game. Always has been, but both college and pro players are now bigger, faster, and stronger than they ever were. The types who used to weigh 250 lbs. now weigh 350 lbs., and the collisions between those 22 athletes on the field are more dangerous now than ever. Sure, the equipment is better now, too, but that might give a false sense of security. With that many bodies flying around at high speed, there are always going to be head injuries, paralyses, and even deaths. A player has to accept those risks, but he shouldn't have to deal with the worst outcome on his own. We need to take care of each other.

The Referee Strike

Speaking of unions, everyone who witnessed the Packers-Seahawks game on September 24, 2012—and one of the worst play calls in NFL history— knows why replacement refs will never be able to take over for the real thing. NFL referees are not just a bunch of Joe Blows off the street. This is a job that takes intelligence and years of experience. Refereeing a game is a complicated and important matter, and replacement refs are just never going to cut it. I think a lot of fans thought, "Well, it's an issue that affects coaches and players, but not me." But the Packers-Seahawks game and other games that were played during the strike proved that it's an issue that affects what fans see on their screens, and certainly affects the outcome of games. Referees are an integral part of the game we love, and if we don't have the best, the quality of NFL broadcasts will decline.

Players Who Commit Crimes

Players who commit crimes should be judged the same as everyone else and go through the system like everyone else. Their treatment should be no more or less harsh than the Average Joe's. Once they've paid the price to society, they should be able to go back and do what they do. I understand the urge to make examples of these athletes, but I don't agree with it. I thought Michael Vick's sentence for dog fighting was too harsh, but I can't deny that the scandal brought attention to a real problem and has probably helped law enforcement make strides in controlling that problem.

I think one of the mistakes people make is expecting professional athletes to be "role models" for themselves and their children. Sure, there will always be a few guys like Kurt Warner and Donald Driver—men who seem to engage in endless charitable giving and are almost seen as saints to the fans—but I still say that if you're counting on the NFL to provide role models for your kids, you're going to be very disappointed. Kids need the people in their real lives to stand up and be their role models, not a bunch of strangers on a flat screen.

How Old Is Too Old to Play Football?

I don't think there is an age that is too old to play football. If you're contributing to the team, you're worth it. It really depends on both the person and the position. The Detroit Lions' kicker Jason Hanson, at age 42, is the oldest active player in the NFL as I write this. I say if he can still play, more power to him. And since I played with 18-year veteran Ed White on the San Diego Chargers, I know that playing with an older, wiser guy can really help some of the youngsters. It's inspirational to see a middle-aged guy who is still doing what he loves.

What about Racism?

You know, I didn't see much of it in college or the NFL, but I'm White. I don't even know if I should be trying to answer this question. If we look at the statistics, we see that African-Americans have made a lot of progress as far as being hired for coaching staffs. And of course it's hard to look at a millionaire pro player and think of him as a victim of anything, no matter his skin color. But when we start talking about black college players, things get more complex, and... Yeah, maybe I shouldn't be the one answering this question.

Women in College and Pro Football

It's silly to me when people act as though this is going to be some big issue in the future, because the vast majority of women will never *want* to play football. But what about those who do? You hear a lot of comments like, "Well, if it's just kicking, I guess that's okay," but I think the rare woman who has the appropriate upper-body strength and talent should be allowed to play any position. Even offensive lineman? Yep, even offensive lineman. And if it psyches out the gentlemen on the opposing team, all the better. Of course, another argument against it is the locker room thing, but would it really be so difficult for an assistant coach at a university to open the women's locker room after a game so a female player could take a shower? I don't think so.

It reminds me of when women reporters first gained access to the locker rooms. The media made such a big deal out of it, and it's true that people in the older generation did some bitching. But I didn't hear one guy my age complaining. We just kept walking around naked. I mean, these were grown women who were there to do a job, and we were grown men who were exhausted after a hard day of work. I can honestly say that sex was the last thing on anybody's mind.

What about the "Gold Diggers"?

Yes, there are lots of women who throw themselves at athletes, but I don't think that excuses the men from anything. They are adults who are able to say no—they just don't want to say no, that's all. This kind of stuff escalates as one goes from high school to college to the pros, and it gets to the point where the "bad stuff" is just being constantly put in front of you. There has to be something within you that guides you in the right direction, or it's really going to make a mess of your life.

As you know from reading the previous chapters, almost nothing was off limits to me when I was young. I was naughty in every other area of life, but for some reason, I was always repulsed by adultery. Don't ask why that was the one issue I took a stand on, but when I saw fellow players cheating on their wives, I was disgusted and made that opinion quite plain to them. And the things I see these days—abandoned illegitimate children, rape— just piss me off even more. These guys need to straighten up and fly right before they start pointing fingers at "gold diggers."

Should Quarterbacks Be Protected More than Other Players?

No. They need to roll with the game just like anyone else. The rules have been changed so much to protect them that I feel like it's affecting the quality of games. But it's pretty pointless of me to even argue this, because it's not going to go my way. Teams have a huge investment in quarterbacks, so they're going to keep doing whatever they have to do to keep them out of harm's way. That's business.

And now that I've taken care of the business of addressing these football issues, back to my issues we go.

CHAPTER TWENTY-THREE

MY LAST DAY ON THE SET of *Heavy* at the Hilton Head Health Institute was rather anti-climactic. Just as they had brought us all in one by one, they let us all go one by one over a period of a week or so. The reason for this was that a director and a camera crew followed each cast member back home in order to film his/her reunions with family and friends. Honestly, I didn't want to leave, and I told everyone working on the show and at the Institute that I would have gladly stayed another month and lost another 142 lbs. How could I not fantasize about staying? Prior to my stint on the show, I'd been homeless and living at Canaan Land, a man without a "real" place to live or a "real" job. My six months at the Institute had been a dream come true, but the whole time I was there, I was wondering and worrying about where on Earth I would go when the time came to leave.

Not for the first time, my former mother-in-law, Kathy Baldus, came to the rescue. Kathy and I had talked during the filming of *Heavy*, and she had asked me where I was planning on living when production shut down. When I said I didn't know, she invited me to come stay with her at her beautiful home in Birmingham, Alabama. Though I'd always known Kathy was a wonderful person, I was still shocked at how loving and generous this offer was. How many moms would give a former son-in-law this kind of chance after he'd caused so much pain and problems for her daughter and grandchild? She even gave me one of her cars to use until I could afford one of my own. Her kind gestures gave me hope that the people around me were really seeing a change in me, and beginning to trust that I would stay on the right path.

My first order of business on the outside was to film my "reveal" with the *Heavy* production crew. Like everything else in this television genre I had thrown myself into, it was kinda real and kinda fake. Filmed at Woody's Senior Night football event in Birmingham, it was staged to look as though I was surprising everyone by showing up. Karen and her sister Kelly *did* know I was coming, but they were surprised by my weight loss, because they had not yet seen me. They were shown tailgating before the game, and then when I came walking through the parking lot, they turned around and the excited looks on their faces were real. We all sat together at the game, and after the game the announcer made my presence known in a booming voice as I walked out onto the field to be reunited with my son. It was so emotional and intense. The show had also filmed me giving a little pep talk to Woody and his teammates at halftime, but that got cut. I didn't care. The really important stuff was there, and I felt my episode ended on a high note and let the viewers know that I was *not* having a relapse, despite those scenes with Natalie.

Before the reveal scenes were taped, I had gone shopping for clothing for the first time since my weight loss, and man, I was like a kid in a candy store. It felt amazing to pull things right off the rack and not even worry about whether I'd be able to find something that fit. I knew I would, and I did. I bought a sports shirt, a sports jacket, and a pair of jeans from a regular department store—not a big and tall men's store. I looked in the store's mirror and I didn't hate myself or want to run off and hide. Mirrors had been my worst enemy for years. I had developed the ability to stand in front of a mirror and see *nothing* but my face. But this time, I forced myself to bend my neck and focus my eyes on my whole body, and I felt fabulous!

Clothes shopping wasn't the only everyday, practical thing to take on a new excitement. Just walking into a nice restaurant and sitting in a chair was a thrill I could have never imagined before this transformation. There was so much more space between my torso and the arms of chairs, whether in restaurants, movie theaters, or stadiums. When you're as big as a small planet and have your own zip code, public activities can be an absolute nightmare. The guy sitting next to you at the theater might grumble or sigh as loudly as possible to express his displeasure about the flesh that is creeping over the chair arms and into his space. And don't even get me started on airplanes. Even as you're walking down the aisle, eyes are rolling as your fellow passengers pray you won't sit next to them and wonder why the obese aren't charged more for a ticket than everyone else is.

But that's one of the weirdest things about being obese: Other than when you're inconveniencing someone else, it's like you're invisible. In this culture where physical perfection and being a "hot" potential sex partner are valued above almost everything else, fat people are the throwaways. Sure, they're somewhat useful if they're willing to go the kooky route and present themselves as entertainment for the thin folks, or if those thin folks can feel superior when they compare and contrast, but other than that, it's as though they're not fully human, with the same needs and desires as everyone else. It had been heartbreaking for me, when I was obese, to see photos of myself back in college, when I was considered a prime physical specimen. Oh, how that handsome young man would have laughed if you'd told him he'd someday be unattractive to the opposite sex.

That's why it was so strange when I left the Institute and I could feel right away that just a little bit of that handsome young man was visible to others again. Women smiled and flirted with me as they hadn't in ages. Men showed me a renewed respect in even the most mundane tasks, like serving me food or taking care of my retail needs. And children no longer seemed quite as intimidated by me, though my height and natural build will probably always make me a little scary to them. That's okay; as soon as I give them a big grin, they're usually just fine. My point is that until you experience such a huge weight loss, you can't really know what a radical effect it has on your life.

Another change that turned out to be more radical than I thought it would be was the simple absence of cameras after I left the Institute. I had loved having the cameras there, and I experienced some anxiety when they were suddenly gone. I missed the attention from the film crew, the producers, the staff at the facility, and the trainers. You would think a middle-aged man would be raring to go and get out into the real world after six months of being constantly observed, poked, prodded, and instructed, but I wasn't. Remember, it hadn't been just those six months. Between Canaan Land and the Institute, my life had been sheltered and controlled for almost four years. I'd been told what to do, what to eat, what to study, what to believe. But now true adulthood was being thrust upon me, and I had to make all my own decisions once again. I couldn't help fearing that I'd make mistakes.

One thing I didn't fear, though, was that I'd put the weight back on. I felt totally in control of that part of my life. I had always known that if I could somehow find a way to devote myself completely to weight loss for a good deal of time, once I got it off I would keep it off. Finally I had found that time, and I was optimistic about the future in that area of my life. I'd redeveloped the good habits I'd had when I was young while keeping the bad habits of my youth at bay, and for that reason I will always feel grateful about being on *Heavy*. I have enough confidence about my ability to control my body that I don't obsess about it; you won't find me on the scale every morning. In fact, I hardly weigh myself at all. I prefer to pay attention to the way I feel and the way my clothing fits. Life is too short to turn yourself into a wreck who's monitoring the numbers on a daily basis.

I was a little lonely in those first weeks after leaving the show. I had been around so many people at all times for years, and it was weird to be alone. Even though I went to live with Kathy as soon as I "got sprung," she had her own life and couldn't be there holding my hand every second of the day. I realized that the best way to be social and make new friends was to model myself after the many people who had helped me on my journey. And who better to help than other men who found themselves in the same trap as I'd been caught in? In Birmingham, I felt the best place to do this would be at Changed Lives Christian Center, a facility where the homeless are allowed to live as they search for jobs and save enough money to reenter society.

Changed Lives works closely with the city of Birmingham to rescue transients who are living dangerous lives in abandoned buildings and under the interstates. Like many cities with warm climates, Birmingham has had a serious homeless problem for decades, which it has addressed with its Ten-Year Plan to Prevent and End Chronic Homelessness. Changed Lives plays a big part in this, with both staff members and volunteers working around the clock to give the best care possible to the men who reside there. I was lucky enough to become a staff member, and before I knew it, I was driving these men to GED test sites and job interviews and sharing as much as I could of my own story with them in order to give them hope. I was really proud to be a part of the Changed Lives crew. Not only do they take care of their residents, they run an outreach medical clinic that provides the homeless who are still on the street with medicine, ointments, eye tests, reading glasses, and toiletries. In this way, they are able to gain the trust of these suffering homeless people, and hopefully bring them into the program at some point.

Working with the staff of Changed Lives and ministering to the residents has made me stronger in my faith. Just like the brash young man I used to be could have never imagined himself as unattractive to women, he also could have never imagined himself taking great pleasure in meeting and befriending "the least of my brothers." Young Bill Searcey just assumed that he would always be part of a rich, fast-living crowd, a guy who had it all. But I now realized that "having it all" in this world could mean absolutely nothing as far as health, happiness, and love. A millionaire's home on Hilton Head Island couldn't stop his death. Wheeling and dealing in real estate couldn't stop a crippling drug addiction. The cachet of two National Championships and a pro football career couldn't stop your wife from leaving you or your friends from finally saying "Enough."

Having it all was no longer what I wanted. Having the most important thing, however—a true faith in God that would guide my time on Earth and give me peace about the world to come—meant everything to me.

CHAPTER TWENTY-FOUR

GOD HAS REACHED DOWN and pulled me out of the fire many times over the years. He did it again in the very beginning of 2012. On New Year's Day, I went to a restaurant for an early dinner with Lisa, my girlfriend at the time. Soon after we ordered, I started feeling bad, like a low blood sugar feeling. I was so hot, and the heat had come over me so fast. "I'm gonna go sit outside for a bit," I told my companion. "I'll be back."

I sat near the entrance to the restaurant and was still sweating so much, even though it was relatively cool outside. I began shaking and my hands began trembling. I tried to psych myself out of it, telling myself it was just low blood sugar, but it just kept getting worse and worse.

Lisa came out to check on me. "You look really pale," she said.

"I don't feel well at all," I replied, "but you go back in and eat. I'll wait out here for you."

"No," she said. "We need to take care of this."

She took me to the local fire department, which was just down the block. The firemen took one look at me and led me into the firehouse, where they pulled my sweatshirt off. Sweat was pouring out of my body and I was trembling uncontrollably. My thoughts were racing: *What now? Why now? What else?* "I've got some chest pain and my shoulder is numb," I told them.

I knew I was having symptoms that were often signs of a heart attack. But, after running an EKG on me, they said, "You don't appear to be having a heart attack, but it could be a stroke or something else."

They put me in an ambulance and rushed me to the hospital. I was feeling worse and worse. At the hospital, a doctor gave me pain medication to calm me and get the situation under control, but I was just not getting better. I knew something was wrong and they knew something was wrong, but no one could figure out what it was. I was very upset, of course, but at least I had one consolation: I'd been working two jobs, and my day job at a real estate company provided me with insurance. At least this treatment would be covered.

Over the next several long, long days, they did all the tests on me that they do when they think someone has a heart problem, including running a wire up my leg and into my heart. They came back with a great report: "Your heart looks fantastic."

"Look, I'm grateful that it's not my heart," I replied, "but I'm telling you, there's a problem here that y'all aren't seeing. It feels like there's an iron rod sticking through my chest."

They ran a CT scan and this time the news wasn't so good: "We found a mass on your left lung. We're sending you to a specialist." Try walking out of a hospital after receiving *that* news. You don't even feel you should be going home; you feel you should be doing something about it *right that very instant*. Instead, you have days, sometimes weeks, to wallow in this information that really doesn't tell you anything except, "You're in big trouble. Not sure how big, but big."

Through all of January, February, and March, I was going through a series of all kinds of tests: x-rays, ultrasounds, MRIs, you name it. That's when they found out that my gall bladder should be removed. Oh, and my pals the kidney stones were back again. And I needed a colonoscopy. I just felt like I was falling apart. First the colonoscopy was performed and they removed some polyps, telling me I'd have to watch that area closely for the rest of my life. Then they removed my gall bladder. Gall bladder surgery is not that big of a deal, but still... another surgery. And all of these problems were just side issues; the tumor was our main concern. Was it cancer?

During this period of uncertainty and confusion, I was frightened in a way that I had never been before. I thought back to all the times I'd come close to death. There was that time I owed a guy money for drugs and was chased though an alley by his "people," bullets whizzing past my head as I jumped into the passenger seat of a getaway car. There was the time I woke up with a gun in my mouth, yet the guy decided not shoot me for some reason. There was the time I took too many pain pills before having knee surgery and almost died on the operating table. There was the homelessness that put me in the line of violence and sickness every single day I was out there. But never had I been so scared as I was now, walking around with this time bomb in my chest.

Then...

Finally...

"Well, it's not cancer..." one doctor told me. *So, it's not a time bomb?* "...but it's growing, it's close to your heart, and I think it's inoperable." *Great, it's still a time bomb.*

I knew I had to find another specialist who could remove this thing. Soon it would be interfering with the function of my heart. At first the new guy thought my thoracic cavity would have to be cranked open like a patient having open heart surgery, but then he and his team decided they could do it robotically, and I initially heaved a sigh of relief. However I realized that at the age of 54, and with my medical background, there were still plenty of reasons to worry.

As always, my son was first and foremost in my thoughts. Was I to die before I really had the chance to redeem myself as a father? I'll admit there was some selfishness on my part; just the thought of dying and never seeing Woody again was my worst nightmare. But once I prayed and got past that, my focus was again on his needs: spiritual, mental, emotional, and financial. Not only did I want to lead him in a faith that would give him eternal rewards, I wanted to make amends right here on earth. In order to do that, I needed more time, but when several of my friends passed away that spring, I wondered if I'd get it. I couldn't stop some dark thoughts from going through my mind. When it's all said and done here on this planet, every one of us is just a coffin and a headstone and box full of legal papers. What is it all about? Did I tell those people that I loved them? Did I try to go back and change any wrongs that I did to them? Did I make the apologies I need to make while I had the chance to make them?

A line of scripture that helped me so much during this rough time was Luke 12:32: *Fear not, little flock; for it is your Father's good pleasure to give you the kingdom.* It's so important for us to remember that the suffering we endure here on earth is a temporary problem. And any time I want to beat any problem, it doesn't hurt to throw in a quote from Coach Bryant, too: "Plan your work, and then work your plan." At first I had kind of thrown up my hands and thought that everything was finally coming to a head; that I was going to go down in flames with lung cancer and kick the bucket relatively quickly (and after all the stuff I'd been through!). But then my faith kicked in and I decided I wasn't going to let it happen without a huge fight, cancer or no cancer.

Good thing I had the tools to hold it together, because troubles just kept piling on. Around the first week in March, Changed Lives Ministry let me know that they were doing away with the full-time, paid position I'd been working at night. They told me I could still live there rent-free if I wanted to get up early in the morning and drive guys to work and make myself available for other ministry stuff. I agreed to this, but was obviously very unhappy that suddenly half my income was gone. Then, within 24 hours, my real estate company told me that they were switching me to a full-time, commission-paying position, and I didn't feel I could handle that in my current situation, so I quit that job. That meant that my insurance would last just long enough to get me through the operation.

When the surgery was successful, and after I'd spent some time recuperating, I realized that some big changes needed to be made in my life. I've moved out of Changed Lives and for the first time in what seems like an eternity, I have my own place, a basement apartment in Birmingham. At this writing, I drive a truck and sweep parking lots for $85 a night. My health problems aren't over; I broke my wrist in three places and can feel some kind of large cyst on my back. The cyst will have to wait, because I no longer have health insurance. But you know what? I believe bigger, better things are coming. I believe that if God's eye is on the sparrow, it is also on me. I'm clear-eyed and sober, and I'm going to stay that way. There's so much left for me to do, because what God will do for one man, he will do for all.

Just days ago, I watched the 2012 National Championship game between Alabama and Notre Dame. I was with some friends and didn't want to cry in front of them, but it wasn't easy to hold back the emotion. As I watched those young men play, I felt none of the negative feelings about myself that I'd felt so many times before. I no longer envied them or wanted to turn back time. I no longer wished that I could be someone else, and not the total loser I was. I no longer saw myself as a bitter, old man who had nothing to offer his fellow human beings. All I wanted now was to show God's love to all my neighbors, and I wondered if my story could have a positive impact on these college athletes who had their whole lives ahead of them. Could they learn something from me?

I know I can't lie to them. I can't try to tell them with a straight face that I never had any fun boozing it up and doing drugs and partying when I was around their age. If I did try to tell them that, thousands of witnesses in Georgia, Alabama, Michigan, Florida, Texas, and California would drown me out with the volume of their mass laughter. No, I can't engage in that kind of hypocrisy. But what I can do—what I'm doing right now—is tell my *whole* story. Be honest about the good times, but make it clear that those good times led to almost complete self-destruction and a sorrow that may never leave me—at least, not in this life.

I know: they're young. They're going to have to learn a lot of lessons all by themselves, through their own trial and error. When I was their age, I didn't want to hear it, either. But when they *are* ready to hear it, I want my words to be true, my arms to be open, my heart to be waiting.

Made in the USA
Lexington, KY
10 June 2015